FOLLOWING THE SHEPHERD

Following the Shepherd

through the twenty-third psalm

Peter Jeffery

EVANGELICAL PRESS OF WALES

© Evangelical Press of Wales, 1996
First published, 1996
ISBN 1 85049 125 9

Cover design and photo by Burgum Boorman Ltd

Published by the Evangelical Press of Wales
Bryntirion, Bridgend CF31 4DX, Wales, UK
Printed by Bridgend Print Centre, Bridgend

Contents

Introduction

Psalm 23 has a special place in the heart of every Christian unrivalled by almost every other portion of Scripture. The depth and beauty of each statement finds either a longing or an echoing response in the believer's heart. The Psalm is one of the most remarkable passages of Scripture because it seems suitable for almost any occasion. Set to music it can be sung with equal suitability at a wedding or a funeral. There is such a breadth to it that it can be applied to most experiences of life.

If there is a problem with these words of David it is that the Psalm is so short that we are tempted not to spend much time studying it, and it is so well known that we assume there is nothing more to learn from it. In my own experience two things shook me out of this complacency. The first was coming across a book on Psalm 23 by John Stevenson published in 1845. The richness of this exposition thrilled my soul and opened my eyes to see and appreciate these familiar words in a new way. The second, was to hear Douglas Mac-Millan preach four remarkable sermons on the Psalm at the Annual English Conference, Aberystwyth, in 1979.[1]

I attempt to write on Psalm 23 in the hope that this book will do for my readers what Stevenson's book and MacMillan's sermons did for me—exalt the Good Shepherd and warm the heart of the sheep.

1 *The Lord our Shepherd* published by the Evangelical Press of Wales, 1983 and still in print.

Introduction

1
The Psalm
of David

David's experience of God in this Psalm is one that every true Christian wants. We all desire to know the Lord leading us, guiding us, providing for us and protecting us. We all want to know rest and peace in life and to fear no evil in our dying moments. These are blessings so desirable that we almost instinctively make Psalm 23 a prayer. But David is not praying here. This Psalm is not a prayer for what David wants but a song of thanksgiving for what he already has.

He is not asking God to do these things for him. He does not say, I hope the Lord will be my Shepherd; he praises God that he already is his Shepherd. David does not theorize about coming to a position at some point in the future when he will lack nothing, but rather delights that because the Lord is his Shepherd he can never lack anything, now or ever. This is the man's experience of God. It is a psalm like this that makes us realize how little we know the Lord. If we are believers we can rejoice in the salvation we have in the Lord Jesus Christ and in that sense we too can say, the Lord is my Shepherd, but do we know the closeness with God that Psalm 23 is obviously describing?

Our experience

The Psalm is the prayer of many Christians, but it is the experience of very few, so how do we make this our experience? We must certainly get beyond merely admiring the beauty of these words of David. There is no doubt that these are magnificent words that flow with an exquisite beauty, but what about the reality of them? The poetic beauty may do something for some cultural or ascetic need we have, but it does nothing for our soul. An ungodly man can be taken up with the beauty of the Psalm, but our privilege as Christians is to experience the reality of the truths expressed here.

The Bible is not a book of lovely thoughts or fanciful theories, it is a book about God and who he is and what he can do for us. What God was to David he wants to be to all his people. David was not a super saint who knew things of God we can never know. Like us all he was a sinner saved by grace. Just like us he often made a mess of his life, but he knew the reality of God, and if we do not know this reality, we need to start by praying for it.

We have to realize that the close fellowship with God described in this Psalm is possible for us. There is a tendency to denigrate ourselves, and think that the rich blessings so often referred to in Scripture are not for ordinary Christians like us. But there is no such thing as an ordinary Christian. Every Christian is the result of a supernatural activity of God the Holy Spirit. We are all the apple of God's eye and precious and honoured in the Lord's sight. It is right to feel unworthy and to to be conscious of our sin, but it is wrong to conclude from this that we are doomed to live second rate spiritual lives.

Sadly, many Christians see the failure in their Christian

lives and get depressed and think they will never know the joy and blessing that David is delighting in. They know the truth of the first statement that the Lord is my Shepherd, that is, they know they have a Saviour. They believe in eternal security and the final perseverance of the saints, so they know the truth of the last statement, I will dwell in the house of the Lord forever. The problem is that somehow all that is in between in the Psalm seems so remote and unreal, and consequently they know little of the present joy and experience of living for God.

Trusting God

The despondent believer makes a sad mistake when he allows his sense of unworthiness, which rightly hinders him from trusting in himself, to prevent him from trusting God. The glory of the gospel is that all the way through it takes into account our unworthiness. The gospel was never meant for great people who are capable and worthy but for poor, wretched sinners. Its message is that Christ died for the ungodly and that to such people God offers a free and full salvation. This salvation includes knowing all the blessings of the love of the Heavenly Father here and now in this world.

If we can truly say the Lord is my Shepherd, then we ought to be able to say everything else in Psalm 23. Really the whole Psalm is a commentary on the first statement. If the Lord is my Shepherd, I cannot lack anything, because he is pledged to look after me. Because he is my Shepherd, he makes me lie down in green pastures, he restores my soul, and so on all the way through the Psalm. Our problem is that we get too preoccupied with ourselves and what we are

achieving, and not preoccupied enough with the Shepherd
and what he has promised to do for us. The message of
Psalm 23 to us is, fix your eyes upon the Lord. The whole
Psalm is about what God does for us, not what we do for
him. David is not one of those believers who is always talking about what he has done for God, Rather he delights in
the Lord and trusts him for all his needs.

The Shepherd's choice

The glory of Psalm 23 is the glory of our privilege as Christians, and we are to rejoice in this. The Lord is the Shepherd,
we are the sheep, and the simple fact is that the Shepherd
chooses the sheep and not the sheep the Shepherd. Or, to be
more accurate, God chooses the sheep and gives them to
Jesus the Good Shepherd (John 10:29). There can be no greater
privilege than that. It was God who made himself David's
Shepherd. Jesse's son did not take upon himself this great
privilege, but God called him and brought him into a living
relationship with himself.

What God did for David, he has done for all his people.
The Lord God in love and mercy has placed himself in relationship to our souls as shepherd to the sheep. There is no
rational explanation for this other than that this is a sovereign act of divine love. It is certainly not that we are more
worthy of God's love than anyone else. He chooses whom
he chooses. There all the argument about the mechanics of
this choice must stop, but the implications of it are vast. Not
least of these is that it humbles us. This doctrine causes us to
see our nothingness, but at the same time there is nothing
like it to lift our spirits and reveal to us the wonder of divine
grace.

Why is it that so many Christians have trouble with the fact of the Shepherd choosing his sheep? Imagine a sheep market with farmers and shepherds milling around intending to increase their flock of sheep. How do they add to their flock? They do not walk past the sheep pens and wait for some animal to bleat its acceptance of them. The sheep do not say, I will have the farmer with the green hat to be my shepherd. That would be absurd. It is the farmer who does the choosing. The sheep are passive: they go where they are told.

If we think it is ridiculous for a sheep to choose a man to be its shepherd, how much more ridiculous is it for a miserable creature like sinful man to choose almighty God. It has to be God who chooses. Whatever else may be true or not true of you as a Christian, it is God who has made you one of the sheep of his flock. And he did so knowing everything about you. He knew your weaknesses and failures, but still he chose you. If when we were his enemies God could love us and choose us, he will not love us any less now that we are one of his sheep. This should encourage us to rejoice that nothing can separate us from the love of God.

We are not to take our sin lightly, and it is right that we should mourn over it, but at the same time, even that sin does not cancel the shepherd/sheep relationship. The Bible teaches us to examine our hearts and to recognize our unworthiness, but it never tells us to stop there. If we stop at our sinfulness, we will never know the riches of God's love and grace. See your sin and unworthiness, but then turn the page over and discover a new and glorious chapter. In spite of your sin there is a God, a Shepherd who never stops loving you. All the worth is on God's side. It always was, and always will be.

Absorbed in God

In Psalm 51 David laments the depth of his sin, but even then he does so against the backcloth of the grace and pardon of a loving God. In this he is like all the Bible writers, as the focus of their attention always comes back to the greatness of God. They delight in the love of God, but there they have a problem. How can they find words adequate enough to describe such love? They employ every phrase expressing human affection to try to describe God's love. They use all sorts of illustrations to show us in some measure the greatness of God's love. But even the most glorious language and most vivid imagery is inadequate for this task. They do their best, and use a great variety of picture language. God is the Rock, the Corner Stone, The Foundation—all to show us something of the immortality of God. Then they change the metaphor: Christ is the Tree of Life, the Root of David, the Righteous Branch, the True Vine. They change the language again and Christ becomes the Light of the World, the Bright and Morning Star, the Sun of Righteousness. Or again, he is the Friend of sinners, our Brother, Father, Husband, Lover of our souls, the Lord our Shepherd. These men, even when inspired by the Holy Spirit to write Scripture, cannot ever come to a final and satisfactory description of God. But God excites them and they are taken up with him. Many of us have problems with prayer. We feel we do not have the words and language others may have, and so we are afraid to pray in public. We need to realize that the most eloquent language is totally inadequate to do justice to our God. We are all alike as Christians, just poor sinners in the presence of a loving Father. Words are not the important thing, but we need to be taken up with God, absorbed in God, delight in God.

In Psalm 23 David is clearly lost in the wonder of his God. He may have been thinking of all the blessings God had brought into his life, and he gropes with words to praise the Lord. His language is simple, not profound. His concepts are not vague and mystical, but common and known to all. He simply says, The Lord is my Shepherd. For him this sums up the character of his God. But the point of the Psalm is that he is engrossed in the Lord, and there is no better place for the believer to be.

David glories in the freeness and fullness of divine grace. He rejoices in the exceeding greatness of God's love, that this Almighty God should condescend to be his Shepherd. The language is simple, but the truth is amazing, and the experience of it is breathtaking. In all the circumstances of life God is providing for me, and even when I make a mess of things, God restores my soul. Every day the goodness and mercy of God follow me to minister to my needs. Death itself, that last enemy which has always terrified man, is even subdued by the presence of the Shepherd. How favoured David was to know these things, but such blessing is not confined to him alone. All Christians are promised this in salvation. Jesus is the Good Shepherd who died for us, and wants us to have life to the full (John 10:13).

The Psalm is meant to show us the greatness of God and the greatness of our privilege as the people of God. If you are a Christian, you are among the most favoured people in the world. You are the most blessed of all people. You may have plenty of problems: David did, but the Lord is your Shepherd, and that outweighs everything else.

2
The Lord is
my Shepherd

The Psalm speaks of David's experience of God and throughout there is an overwhelming sense of reality. It is clear that the Psalmist is speaking of a God he knows, and in doing so he reveals the great joy in his heart brought about by the real and close communion he has with God. The Lord is my shepherd speaks of nearness and involvement, of concern and dependence. It reveals to us what the Lord our God can be to every believer, and ought to be in the experience of all his people.

The Lord

To appreciate fully the wonder of what David is saying, we need to see that the emphasis is on the word 'Lord', not 'shepherd'. It is who the Shepherd is that is remarkable. Who is David's shepherd? When in Scripture the title for God is all in capital letters as Lord is here, it means that the original Hebrew word is Jehovah. This is the greatest title by which God revealed himself to man. Jehovah is the great name which the Old Testament is always delighting in. In Psalm 83 the psalmist says of the enemies of God, 'Let them know that you whose name is the Lord (Jehovah)—that you alone are the Most High over all the earth' (v.8). He is a God of all power, one not to be trifled with. Isaiah in chapter 57 delights in the Lord as the high and lofty one, who lives forever and whose name is holy. This is the same Jehovah that Paul calls in 1 Timothy, the eternal King (1:17), and again in Romans 16, the eternal God (v.16).

Throughout the Old and New Testaments the Lord is represented as the one who created the universe out of nothing and upholds it with the word of his own power and the strength of his own hand. This is Jehovah, and this great and glorious creator of the universe has graciously condescended to draw near to David and to all his people.

Shepherd

In the Old Testament the job of shepherd was a most menial one. If a man had several sons it was the youngest who looked after the sheep. David himself was the youngest of Jesse's sons and that was why he was a shepherd. What right did David , or any of us, to call the holy sovereign God his shepherd? Indeed, is it not something of a comedown to refer to so majestic and awesome a being in this way? The answer to both questions is that the title of Shepherd is one that the Lord had given to himself! David did not invent it, nor did he refer to his Lord as Shepherd because he himself happened to be a shepherd. If he had been a fisherman or a shopkeeper, he would have still used this title, because from the earliest times in Scripture the Lord had revealed himself to his people under the picture of a shepherd.

In Genesis 49:24 we find the dying Jacob speaking to his children and reminding them that their God is the Shepherd, and Rock of Israel. Isaiah, in chapter 40, is likewise reminding

Israel who their God is. There is always the tendency to forget the greatness of the Lord, and twice the prophet rebukes the people, 'Do you not know? Have you not heard?' (vv.21 & 28). He then paints a marvellous picture of the greatness of God as the one who sits upon the circle of the earth and before whom the nations are like a drop in a bucket. In the midst of these thrilling words the Lord is described as tending his flock like a shepherd (v.11).

Ezekiel tells us that there are false shepherds who would lead the people of God astray. Nevertheless, the Lord says, 'I myself will search for my sheep and look after them' (34:11). Then God goes on to say, 'I will place over them one shepherd, my servant David, and he will tend them; he will tend them and be their shepherd' (v.23). The David in this verse is not the king who wrote Psalm 23, but David's greater son, the Lord Jesus Christ. Ezekiel is prophesying of the coming of the Messiah, as too is Zechariah (13:7), 'Awake, O sword, against my shepherd . . . strike the shepherd, and the sheep will be scattered.' The day before Calvary, Jesus quoted this verse and applied it to his death on the cross (Matthew 26:31).

The Good Shepherd

The title that David uses to describe his relationship with God was no chance expression arising out of his own particular background. It was a divinely ordained title and there was only one who possessed the right to it. The title was claimed by Jesus when in John 10 he described himself as the Good Shepherd. And the Holy Spirit exclusively applied the title to Jesus when he inspired the writer of Hebrews to call the Saviour the Great Shepherd (13:20) and the Apostle Peter to refer to Jesus as the Chief Shepherd (1 Peter 5:4).

Jesus is the promised Messiah. He is Jehovah, the Lord God, who became flesh at Bethlehem. The Old Testament writers delight in God as their Shepherd and this picture finds its fulfilment in the Lord Jesus Christ. Jesus is our Shepherd. The one who died on the cross did so as our Shepherd giving his life for the sheep. Jesus from the beginning of time is the only Shepherd of God's flock. He is the self-existing, uncreated, eternal Jehovah whose love and care, providence and power, are unlimited and inexhaustible.This is why Christians always need to be diligent in maintaining the doctrine of the Person of Christ. He is no mere man, but God incarnate. If Jesus is not God, then he is not our Shepherd. And if he is not our Shepherd, then we are lost, both now in this world and for all eternity in hell. But Jesus is God. He is Jehovah. He is our Shepherd, and his Shepherd care extends over all time and eternity. He is the Shepherd to all the saints in every generation, supplying their need, and anticipating every emergency, and ensuring the happiness and security of every single member of the flock.

Dependable

The Shepherd has the ultimate responsibility for the flock. If he is to lead it into green pastures, he has to first find those pastures. The same is true about the quiet or still waters. So the flock has to depend for its very existence and survival upon the Shepherd. Is such a dependence justified? Yes, it is totally justified because the Shepherd is Jesus. In strength he is almighty, in wisdom he is omniscient, in love he is unequalled, and in resources he is unbounded. There are no evils that he cannot deal with; no dangers that he cannot avert; no enemy that he cannot defeat, and no needs that he cannot supply.

No wonder David delights in his Shepherd and the same is true of all believers. All we need we can find in Jesus. To the troubled heart he can bring peace, to the weary rest, to the penitent pardon, to the weak strength. Christians lose so much of the joy of salvation by concentrating on what they can do for the Shepherd instead of on what the Shepherd has done and continues to do for them.

The flock is the constant object of his love. He knows every sheep and lamb by name. No human shepherd could be like that. But Jesus has our names engraved on the palms of his hands. There is not a second when his eye wavers from us, not a moment when his prayers and intercession desert us. He sees us all as individuals and loves us with an everlasting love. Therefore the greatest privilege any human being can have is to know Jesus as their Shepherd.

The Lord is my Shepherd is an amazing statement and everything else in the Psalm follows on as an inevitable consequence of it. This is not some theoretical proposition. It is not wishful thinking: it is far more even than just a theological statement. This is the experience of all God's people. This is what we are saved to, and the reality of what we are saved to is known as we submit to the care of the Shepherd. It is no use saying the Lord is my Shepherd, and then worrying myself sick about where I am going to find green pastures. If the green pastures and quiet waters are found as a result only of our efforts, we don't need a Shepherd. But the fact is we make a terrible mess of life, and we need Jesus to be our Shepherd.

3
He provides for me

David claims that because the Lord is his Shepherd he will lack nothing. He is saying that there is no possible situation in which he will be in need. In any day and age this is a remarkable statement. After all, it is no millionaire making this claim but a poor shepherd boy. And even if he was a millionaire, we may think the assertion could almost be tempting providence, because history is full of millionaires who became bankrupt.

We are living in days when most folk are dissatisfied, and believe they need 101 different things to make life palatable. Almost the whole advertising industry is based on this sense of dissatisfaction, and seeks to create in people's minds a desire for something they do not need. The ads work so well that we are convinced we desperately need such and such a product. David did not have to put up with advertising brain washing, but he did have to confront the greed that is in every sinful heart. In spite of this, he can make the amazing statement, I shall lack nothing.

The basis for his claim

David was no fool, and he realized how uncertain and

chequered life can be. He could calmly contemplate the changes and chances of this very uncertain world, and yet still say these words. His claim is made simply on the basis of the fact that the Lord is his shepherd. He does not say it on the grounds of wealth, ability or future prospects, but upon the ground of his living relationship with the eternal God.

Here is a man whose experience of God is not superficial or nominal, but real and deep. If we are honest with ourselves, most of us have difficulty with this claim. We, of course, as Christians believe it in theory, but are not actually prepared to make it a principle to build our lives upon. The reason for this is the shallowness of our experience of God. We can say the Lord is my Shepherd, because we know that the only hope we have of salvation is that the Good Shepherd gave his life for the sheep. We heard his voice calling us through the message of the gospel, and in repentance and faith we came to him for pardon. All this we can rejoice in, but actually trusting the Shepherd day by day in the problems and necessities of life is quite another thing.

For the Christian the Lord as our Shepherd ought to be the foundational factor of our life, and the whole of our life should be built upon this great truth. If the Lord is my Shepherd, then he is responsible for my provision and safety. How can I possibly lack anything if the Lord God Almighty is responsible for my needs? This is one of the necessities of faith, and the Christian is under an obligation to believe that the Lord will never let him down. Not to believe that is to insult the character and honour of our Shepherd.

When David claims that he will lack nothing, he does not mean that prosperity and abundance will always be his portion. He is not advocating a health and wealth and prosperity gospel. He does not say life will be all sweetness and roses with no difficulties and heartaches. Neither is he claiming that he will always have the best job and biggest house. In fact he is making no positive statement at all. I shall lack nothing, is a negative statement. He does not presume to guess at what his earthly circumstances will be, but whatever they are, he is confident of the loving care of his God. Whatever life may hold, troubles or blessings, he knows that his heavenly Shepherd will withhold nothing that would be needful for his spiritual or physical well being.

The claim is very similar to that of Paul in Philippians 4. The apostle says, whatever the circumstances of life, he has learnt to be content. He will not let circumstances dictate how he is going to live his Christian life. Circumstances can be a very powerful influence upon us, and if we let them dominate our thinking and attitudes, then we are behaving exactly as an unbeliever behaves. Agur, in writing Proverbs 30, prays about two extremes of circumstance. 'Two things I ask of you, O Lord . . . give me neither poverty nor riches, but give me only my daily bread' (vv.7 & 8). In verse 9 he gives the reason for this request, 'Otherwise, I may have too much, and disown you, and say, Who is the Lord? Or I may become poor and steal, and so dishonour the name of my God.'

His fear is that prosperity will cause him to be self-sufficient and forget his need of God, or that poverty may equally cause him to forget the promises of God and lead him to meet his own needs by stealing. This prayer of Agur furnishes us with a good exposition of the meaning of, 'I shall lack nothing'. David says, I may not be over-rich or know the extremity of poverty, but whatever my circumstances my eye is always upon God. My cheque book will not solve my problems, neither will acts of dishonesty; God alone is my sufficiency.

This claim is based not upon vain self-confidence or misplaced enthusiasm, but wholly upon the grace and power of the one he calls his Shepherd. God, he says, shall meet my needs.

Needs

I shall lack nothing means that I will never be short of what I really need. Need is always a relative term. A man accustomed to very little may think that if he has a £20 note he is rich. Another man accustomed to plenty would consider £20 a very small sum, because he thinks in terms of thousands. A man used to little can be satisfied with little, compared with the man used to plenty. So people can convince themselves they are in need, when at the same time they are in possession of more than enough to satisfy the necessities of life. Many Christians in the western world may feel they are in need, but if someone living in India had a fraction of what we have he would consider himself wealthy.

There is a great difference between what we need and what we want, and the Christian must not allow himself to be influenced by the false values of the world. A Christian can be poor in financial terms and yet still not be in need. One of the marks of the humanity of our Saviour is that he was poor. We are told he had nowhere to lay his head. He was always poor, but never in need, because he lived dependent upon the providential care of his Heavenly Father. Jesus never performed a miracle to meet his bodily needs. He did miracles to meet the physical needs of others, and fed 5,000 and 4,000 in a miraculous way. But when he was hungry in John 4, he sent his disciples into the city to buy food. He looked not to the miraculous but to the common grace of God.

If God chooses to withhold certain things from us, things that we may want but not need, then the contented mind accepts this. Someone has said that a contented mind has a continual feast. If we had that sort of attitude to life, then ninety per cent of our anxieties and worries would disappear. Many of our problems are not ones of material lack but of wrong attitudes. If lust instead of contentment dominates our thinking, it is because we have never really understood what it means to have the Lord as our Shepherd.

When as Christians we grumble about wanting things, what is really happening is that the sheep are taking over the job of the shepherd. Our lips may affirm that the Lord is our Shepherd, but our lusts and anxieties and fears deny it. We speak as if we love him and worry as if we cannot trust him.

It is unhealthy for a Christian to trust God with his immortal soul but not with his mortal, bodily needs. We believe that salvation is all of grace and that we contribute nothing to our justification, so we rest totally in God for our eternal welfare. Yet we are reluctant to trust this same God for the needs of our bodies which will only last for 70 or so years. That has got to be wrong. David's words in Psalm 23 apply to all our needs, both spiritual and physical. We shall look at the spiritual provisions of the Shepherd in later chapters, but here we consider his provisions for our physical needs.

The Shepherd is concerned about the welfare of his sheep. He wants to know them and feed them and protect them from their enemies. He is concerned with everything about them, so the love of God embraces all our needs. In some ways it is easier to rejoice that we will dwell in the house of the Lord for ever, but we must also learn to rejoice in God's promises for this life. This does not encourage the irresponsible attitude that is sometimes embodied in the glib way

some Christians use the phrase, 'the Lord will provide'. Paul
warns the Thessalonians against idleness with the stark statement, 'if a man will not work, he shall not eat' (2 Thessalonians 3:10). Irresponsibility is no part of the Christian life,
but neither is over-anxiety. Both stem from a wrong view of
the relationship of shepherd and sheep.

Trusting the Shepherd

What David believed about God in Psalm 23 was constant
throughout his life. Like us all, he may have had moments
when his eye wandered from the divine provider, but the
general tenor of his life was to trust God. So this statement in
Psalm 23 is not unusual for him. For instance, in Psalm 33:19
he speaks of the unfailing love of God that works for his
people to 'keep them alive in famine'. In Psalm 34 we read in
verses 9 and 10, 'Fear the Lord, you his saints, for those who
fear him lack nothing. The lions may grow weak and hungry,
but those who seek the Lord lack no good thing.' The mighty
lion, the king of the jungle, that trusts in its own powers of
cunning and strength might find itself in great need, but not
those people whose trust is in the Lord.

Statements like these should be a great encouragement to
all believers. They are not confined only to the Old Testament. Hebrews 13:5-6 urges us to, 'Keep your lives free from
the love of money and be content with what you have,
because the Lord has said, "Never will I leave you; never will
I forsake you".' To such a promise there can only be one response—'So we say with confidence, "The Lord is my helper;
I will not be afraid. What can man do to me?"' Because God
makes such promises to us, it is wrong that we should ever
worry about our material needs. In the Sermon on the

Mount, Jesus warns us against being over anxious (Matthew 6:25-34). His argument is very simple—your heavenly Father knows what you need, and you can trust him to supply it.

Not to trust is evidence of a small faith that may believe God is able to meet our needs but is not sure if he is willing. Jesus is not condemning people for planning for the future. It is one thing to plan for next week, but quite another to worry about next week. Anxiety is sin, because it denies the truth of Psalm 23, 'I shall lack nothing'. It is the sin of not trusting God. It may be objected, I cannot help worrying. Of course we can help it. To say that is to deny that anything significant happened to us in our salvation. It is true that some folk are by temperament more prone to worry than others, but whatever our temperament, we as Christians have every reason to trust the Lord our Shepherd.

If we do not trust Christ and go our own way, we will find ourselves in trouble and probably in need. The reason will not be that the Shepherd has stopped providing, but that we have stopped following him. It is possible for us never to waver in trusting Christ with our souls, but at the same time not to trust him for other things. Trusting the Shepherd does not mean, as we have seen, sitting back and doing nothing. We need to be wise and diligent in ordering our lives; we need to work and be industrious, because the Lord will not bless laziness. The book of Proverbs is full of this. 'Laziness brings on deep sleep, and the shiftless man goes hungry' (19:15). 'A sluggard does not plough in season; so at harvest time he looks but finds nothing' (20:4).

We are to meet our responsibilities, to work and plan in a biblical and legitimate way, but that is totally different from being over-anxious. Trusting the Lord is a most reasonable exercise, and we have incentives to do so all around us. The birds, the fields and flowers, says Jesus, all have their needs met by God, and you are of more value than they are. If we look back in our lives, we will see many difficult times when trials and sorrows seem to have piled up against us. We did not like those experiences, and probably moaned loudly and complained bitterly. But looking back now we can see the hand of God in it all. Not for a moment did he leave us alone. So trust him now in present problems.

In all probability, when we read such a statement as David's we can think of many fine Christians who have been overwhelmed with needs and difficulties, and we begin to doubt the truth of, 'I shall lack nothing'. It is true that there are many perplexing things that happen to us in this life, but we need to hang on to the great unchanging truth that the Lord is our Shepherd. If he is our Shepherd we shall lack nothing of the necessities of life. We may feel deeply that this is not so, but before we accuse God, perhaps we ought to examine ourselves. Am I lacking what I need or merely what I want? Have I truly been trusting God to meet my needs? Perhaps the Lord is not giving us what we think we need but something else instead, something more wonderful. God did not answer Paul's prayer by removing his thorn in the flesh, but he did promise that 'my grace is sufficient for you' (2 Corinthians 12:9). Perhaps the Lord is allowing us to face certain problems to teach us more of his love?

Whatever our experience may be, the Lord is still our Shepherd and he cares about us.

4
He feeds my soul

David paints for us here a picture of the sheep lying down, not on some barren hillside where the grass is withered and lacking in nourishment, but in the tender grass, the green grass that will do it the most good. The sheep may in its rebellion wander into the barren area, but it is not led there by the shepherd.

From this simple illustration, David points us to the concern the Lord our Shepherd has to feed and nourish our souls. As Christians we may wilfully go into areas of life where there is nothing but spiritual barrenness, and the inevitable results will be seen in our lives, but the Shepherd will not lead us to such places. This is one way to test guidance. How do I know is the Lord is leading me in a particular matter? I can ask myself, is the direction I am going doing my spiritual life good? Is my soul being nourished? Is my prayer life being enriched? If so, then in all probability the Lord is leading me. But if I find myself somewhere where my soul is being starved of the bread of life, then I can be sure that is not where the Lord wants me to be.

The Psalmist describes for us the fullness and richness of the spiritual provision the Christian can enjoy under the pastoral care of Jehovah, the Lord our Shepherd. God's love and grace are seen in the words, 'he makes me'. The provision is his and the 'make' is not that of compulsion but of privilege.

Apart from the Lord providing, there would be no food for our souls. All the rich experiences of spiritual refreshment would be nothing but a fairy story to us; something we may have heard of but never known for ourselves. Our Shepherd gives us both a taste for spiritual riches, and also leads us into those places where we can actually enjoy them.

The green pastures of Scripture

Some of the richest green pastures are found in Scripture and God feeds our souls pre-eminently upon the truth of his Word. As tender green grass is able to nourish and sustain the natural life of a sheep, so the Bible, uniquely, is able to preserve and strengthen the spiritual life of every child of God. The field of Holy Scripture is a green and ample pasture to feed in. It is fresh and pleasant, rich and varied, suitable and satisfying, and this is because the Bible is the depository of eternal and divine truth. Jesus tells us in Matthew 4:4, 'Man does not live on bread alone, but on every word that comes from the mouth of God.' Separate from the Word of God our spiritual life would wither, shrink, become sickly and unhealthy.

One of the objectives of Scripture is to counteract the lies of Satan. Jesus said (John 8:44) that the Devil is the father of lies, and the purpose of these lies is to lead God's sheep astray. As light is to darkness, medicine is to disease and life is to death, so is the truth of God to the lies of Satan. The Devil is no fool, and his are lies not always easy to spot. He is the master of delusion, guile and deceit, and many a believer has been led into disastrous paths by not recognizing the source of the lead he follows. But Jesus said, 'The words I have spoken to you are spirit and they are life' (John 6:63). If we value our souls we will listen to the words of Jesus and to the whole of divine revelation as found in Scripture. It is only in the Bible that we find the truth of God. It is true that we can see something of the glory of God in nature. But you do not see the saving love and grace of God in a flower or a tree. You do not know God as Saviour from creation. These truths you find in Scripture as Jesus is revealed to us in all his beauty and fullness. This is why Jesus told us to search the Scriptures, because in them we will find him, and this is also why Paul said the Scriptures are able to make us wise for salvation.

In Psalm 12:6 David tells us that, 'the words of the Lord are flawless, like silver purified in a furnace of clay, purified seven times.' Seven is always the biblical figure for perfection, and when David says the words of the Lord are like silver purified seven times, he is speaking of its perfection. The Word of the Lord is reliable and trustworthy. It is pure food for our souls and we cannot exist without it. Here are the treasures of mercy and grace, of pardon and peace, of love and joy. This is the divinely appointed food for the soul of the Christian, and he cannot exist in a healthy state without feeding on it. This is the green pasture we are to feed in. Can you imagine a shepherd leading his flock to lush green grass, but the sheep stubbornly refusing to eat? What would the sheep be like in a week if they do not eat? Would they be able to survive a month if their stubbornness persists? A Christian who does not feed on the green pasture of Scripture is in the same plight. His spiritual life will weaken and the health of his soul will deteriorate rapidly. It is inevitable because Scripture is essential to our spiritual well being. In Psalm 19 David lists some of the vital ingredients for a healthy spiritual life. What is it that brings great reward to the people of God? It is by giving serious and earnest attention to the law of God which revives the soul, the statutes of the Lord which make wise the simple, and the precepts of the Lord which give joy to the heart (read the whole of Psalm 19). This is what Scripture does for the Christian. It does not do it for the non-Christian, because he cannot understand or digest the things of God. But the believer is one who has been given an appetite and taste for divine truths. For such a man to neglect the provisions of God is the height of folly.

The green pastures of the Church

The Lord our Shepherd has more than one pasture to feed his flock. There are also the pastures of prayer, fellowship and ministry that all do immense good in promoting our spiritual growth. David said, 'I rejoiced with those who said to me, let us go to the house of the Lord' (Psalm 122:1). He rejoiced because he knew that the house of the Lord was going to be green pasture for his soul. There he would meet with others of the redeemed and praise the Lord for his goodness. There prayer and ministry would enrich his soul. Do you wake up on Sunday morning with David's joy in your heart? Listen to another of the Psalmists, 'How lovely is your dwelling place, O Lord Almighty! My soul yearns, even faints for the courts of the Lord' (Psalm 84:1). Here was a man who knew where the green pastures were and he couldn't wait to feed in them. How often has a believer come to God's house dry and barren, low and depressed, but gone away rejoicing? Fellowship, worship and the preaching of Scripture has refreshed the downcast soul. That is no accident, but part of the Shepherd's love for his sheep. It is not the church building or even attending a service, but God by his Holy Spirit feeding our souls that brings about the transformation. This is why the Lord has given us his day and why he commands us not to forsake the gathering together. This is why Jesus set us the example of being in the synagogue every Sabbath day. The church is one of the great blessings God has given us. It is not something invented by man for religious ceremonies, but it is ordained by God for the good of his people. In church God is known and felt and loved. His presence is realized, his faithfulness proved. his power experienced again, and his mercy enjoyed. It is not only in church that we know these things, but most certainly we experience them there because the house of God is green pasture to our souls.

This is one of the reasons why the Devil will always seek to keep a believer from attending church on a Sunday. Have you ever found yourself feeling spiritually low and thinking it is not worth going to church in that frame of mind? You think that you will not get anything out of it, so why not stop away? That may sound reasonable, but it is totally wrong. The more miserable you feel, the more reason you have to go to God's house, because that is the place where God can put you right. Asaph in Psalm 73 felt low and depressed, and began to wallow in self-pity. He saw the injustices of life, evil men prospering and the good suffering. He came to the conclusion that faith in God was a waste of time (v.13). He was confused and bewildered until he went to the sanctuary of God, and there the eternal truths of God began to feed his soul. Understanding and faith were rekindled as God met with him.

Lying down

The provisions of God to meet our spiritual needs are so rich and constant that it is amazing that Christians ever get into a state of spiritual barrenness. Why is it that there is such a thing as a weak Christian? The answer is in the words 'lie down'. God provides the green pastures, but it is our duty and privilege to feed on it, and thus benefit from it. Psalm 63:5-6 help us to understand what it means to lie down in the green pastures. 'My soul will be satisfied as with the richest of foods; with singing lips my mouth will praise you.' When will this spiritual feast be experienced? The next verse tells us, when I think and meditate on you.

Lying down means meditating, thinking, giving time to the things of God. Meditation is the lying down of the soul, the chewing over and digesting of the green pastures. Whenever you see a field of sheep, you can almost guarantee what they will be doing. They will be heads down, all nibbling away at the green grass. They have more sense than some Christians. They do not waste time debating whether or not this grass tastes better than the grass they had last week. The food is there for them, so they get on and enjoy it. The more we eat and the more time we give to thinking and meditating on the things of God, the more we will find our souls built up and strengthened. For instance, the more you think and ponder on God's love for you, the more fervent will grow your love for him. The infinite obligations we see in the gospel lay us under an infinite debt of gratitude: we realize how much we owe God. We feel we cannot love him as we ought, we feel we cannot praise him as we ought, but we do praise him, and the more we praise, the more we love him. This is lying down and feeding on the green pastures. It is giving time to God, not rushing our devotions, but pondering on the glories of the Lord. Then divine love and holy satisfaction fill our hearts, enabling us to know something of what David knew in Psalm 23.

Meditation is the eating and digesting of the green pasture. Without this you can stand in the most lush spiritual pastures and be weak and pathetic. You can have all the translations of the Bible on your shelf; you can sit each week under faithful, powerful, biblical preaching; you can be in a church where there is warm fellowship, but you will not grow spiritually unless you lie down and feed on what the Lord is setting before you.

Have Christians forgotten how to meditate? Are we so busy that our devotional life gets so rushed that it becomes meaningless? Is it perhaps with many Christians their whole devotional life takes place within the four walls of their place of worship, and outside of church they never pray and never open the Bible? The weakness of the Christian church at the end of the twentieth century is due essentially to the weakness of the individual Christians who make up the church, and the weakness of the believers has got to be due to the fact that we do not make the most of the green pastures our Shepherd provides for us.

Meditation means giving time, and giving time means taking it from somewhere else. There is a desperate need for us all to re-assess our priorities. The writer to the Hebrews rebukes his readers because they were slow to learn (Hebrews 5:11). They had been Christians for several years and by this time should have been teaching others, but this was not possible because they were still spiritual infants. Solid food was available to them, but instead they fed on milk. The result was a stunted spiritual growth. Verse 14 goes on to say, 'solid food is for the mature, who by constant use have trained themselves to distinguish good from evil.' 'Constant use' and 'train themselves' imply that time and discipline and effort were given to the study of the Word of God.

Is your soul hungry? Is there a leanness and dryness in your spiritual life? Then the answer is to feed on the green pastures. The Shepherd provides the food—so eat, digest, ponder and enjoy the rich and varied diet the Lord provides for you. Lie down and take time to soak up the goodness of God.

5
He refreshes me

The Shepherd of our souls, unlike a human shepherd, has a flock so vast that no man could count the sheep. He has set out to conduct his flock to the heavenly promised land without the loss of a single sheep or one feeble lamb. None will be lost and considering the nature of sheep to stray, that is an amazing undertaking.

The territory of this world, that the Shepherd is taking the sheep through, is a graveyard for the souls of men and women. Everything in it can be hostile to the Christian's spiritual progress and it would be impossible for him to survive without the Shepherd's guidance and leading. The wilderness of the world provides no food for the Christian's soul, no refreshment for the one whose desire is to please God. It is only by the utmost tenderness and vigilance on the part of our Shepherd that there is any hope of us reaching heaven. But reach it we will, because the Lord has promised to lead us all the way.

The Shepherd never leads his flock by the broad highways of glamour and tinsel that the world is so fond of. Neither does he lead down the road of easy religion, but always by the narrow path of righteousness. Running parallel to this narrow way is a stream of refreshing grace, the quiet waters that Psalm 23 refers to.

Spiritual refreshment

Each statement of the Psalm is meant to convey a spiritual truth, so what does it mean to teach us when it says the Shepherd leads us beside quiet waters? Throughout Scripture water is used as a symbol of the work and ministry of the Holy Spirit. We see this for instance in Isaiah 44:3, 'For I will pour water on the thirsty land, and streams on the dry ground. I will pour out my Spirit on your offspring, and my blessing on your descendants.'

David is speaking here of the heavenly peace and inward calm that is the privilege of the Christian to enjoy through the ministry of the Holy Spirit. Quiet or still waters is a beautiful expression and depicts for us the peaceful and blessed state of the believer whose spirit is constantly being refreshed by the Holy Spirit. The Lord never leads his people into circumstances in which it is impossible for them to obtain the enlivening and refreshing influences of the Spirit. If we follow that lead, even though the path may be hard, there will always be the quiet waters for us to drink in. But if we rebel and go our own way, then spiritual barrenness and dryness will be the result.

Like all waters, the quiet waters have a source from which they flow. The Holy Spirit proceeds from the Father and the Son. In Revelation, John speaks of the river of the water of life that flows from the throne of God and of the Lamb (22:1). In John 15, Jesus is preparing his Apostles on the night before his death for the fact that he is to leave them. He encourages them in the face of such devastating news with the promise to send the Holy Spirit to them, 'the Spirit of truth, who goes out from the Father' (verse 26).

In Scripture, the presence and operation of the Holy Spirit

in the heart of the Christian is constantly spoken of as water. Jesus said, 'Whoever believes in me, as the Scripture has said, streams of living water will flow from within him. By this he meant the Spirit' (John 7:38-39). This stream is quiet, deep and steady in its flow. This is different from the babbling brook or the rushing torrent, which are generally shallow and uncertain in their course. They come rushing down the hillside and the sheep will not drink in them. The quiet water glides slowly and gently forward, as if unwilling to pass on until all its refreshing blessings have been imparted on every side. This is the Holy Spirit's ministry in the heart of the Christian.

It is true that sometimes in the Bible the Spirit is spoken of under other symbols. For instance, the opposite to water would be fire, and at Pentecost the Holy Spirit is spoken of as tongues of fire. So there are different aspects of the Spirit's work, but when he is referred to as water, what is generally meant is the refreshing, fertilizing, quenching, cleansing and softening ministry that the heart of every believer needs. The Spirit satisfies the thirst we have for God and softens the hardness of our stubborn hearts. Sometimes God has to cause us to tremble as the message of the fire of the law is applied to us by the Holy Spirit , but even then the quiet waters are not far away. God will rebuke his people if it is necessary, but he does not delight in this. His delight is in refreshing us. The soul that thirsts for support amidst troubles and tribulation finds peace and refreshment in the ministry of the Spirit to his heart. The Holy Spirit may use the Scriptures, and what a thrill it is when the Word of God speaks to a special problem we are wrestling with. At other times in our despair the Lord draws near by his Spirit. He comes himself to refresh us, and there is nothing quite like this. In the midst of barrenness, we are refreshed as we feel and know the presence of the Shepherd.

When hope seems to depart and all appears dark and gloomy, how does God minister to us? Listen to Romans 15:13? 'May the God of hope fill you with all joy and peace as you trust in him, so that you may overflow with hope by the power of the Holy Spirit.' Joy, peace and hope are the products of trusting God. They are not a reward, but the inevitable results of a Christian life knowing the refreshing influences of God the Holy Spirit at work in it.

Living in the fear of the Lord

Joy, peace and hope are blessings that all believers want to enjoy, but the New Testament also encourages us to live our lives in the fear of the Lord. This is not the fear of terror or uncertainty, but of awe, wonder and respect. Many of our problems as Christians stem from the fact that we take God for granted and begin to play fast and loose with him. In other words, we lose the sense of the fear of the Lord, and spiritually this is disastrous.

After a time of bitter persecution we are told in Acts 9:31 that the church enjoyed a time of peace. The peace was not simply because the persecution became less intense but that the Holy Spirit brought them again to the still waters and ministered to them in his unique way. We read in the same verse that the church 'was strengthened and encouraged by the Holy Spirit, it grew in numbers, living in the fear of the Lord.' The key to most things in the Christian life is whether or not our attitude to God is correct, whether or not we are living in the fear of the Lord. If we are, then persecution or no persecution, hard times or the smooth paths, we will know the Holy Spirit strengthening us. He leads us by the quiet waters not only to refresh us but to help us catch again a glimpse of the greatness and majesty of our God. This surely is the greatest refreshment for a redeemed soul.

The Christian life is a spiritual walk; a life lived according to the leading of the Holy Spirit. Romans 14:17 tells us that, 'the kingdom of God is not a matter of eating and drinking, but of righteousness, peace and joy in the Holy Spirit.' These blessings are not for special times, they are meant to be the normal experience of the people of God. When God saved us he turned an enemy into a child; he changed a situation of antagonism into one of fellowship. We are saved to have fellowship with God. But this is only possible on the merit of Jesus our Good Shepherd, and under the influence and guidance of the Holy Spirit. If as Christians our hearts are dry and barren and we feel that God is a million miles away, it is because we have wandered away from the Shepherd, and the quiet waters of spiritual nourishment are only a memory.

The answer to such a terrible condition is not to seek a spiritual experience as if the Holy Spirit will wave a magic wand and everything will be alright again. The answer is to begin to live again in the fear of the Lord; to take God seriously and follow the leading of the Spirit as he begins to put his finger of accusation on sins in your life. God wants you back at the quiet waters. But do you want to be there? David put it like this in Psalm 63, 'my soul thirsts for you, my body longs for you, in a dry and weary land where there is no water' (v.1). For a Christian any experience other than being close to the Shepherd is a dry and weary one, and surely then the greatest longing should be for the Lord himself.

Being led

The Christian gets soul satisfaction when he is following the lead of his Shepherd. One of the problems we are constantly having to battle with is the desire to do our own thing. This is a disease of modern society that we must resist with great determination. Thank God that our Shepherd will restore us when we make a mess of things, but it is our responsibility not to get into a mess in the first place. The only way to achieve this is to follow the lead we are given.

God's leading will not always take us down smooth paths but they will always be paths where we have access to the quiet waters. 'Then will the lame leap like a deer, and the tongue of the dumb shout for joy. Water will gush forth in the wilderness and streams in the desert' (Isaiah 35:6). Here the prophet is describing God providing for the spiritual needs of his people when they are in a wilderness experience. He does the same thing in chapter 41:17-18, 'The poor and needy search for water, but there is none; their tongues are parched with thirst. But I the Lord will answer them; I, the God of Israel, will not forsake them. I will make rivers flow on barren heights, and springs within the valleys. I will turn the desert into pools of water, and the parched ground into springs.'

The quiet, still, refreshing waters of spiritual nourishment are not ones we stumble upon by accident, but ones the Shepherd leads us to. We need to drink deeply of these waters. They may not be as exciting as the rushing streams, but they do our souls more good. The Shepherd leads, so let us follow eagerly and in expectation.

6
He restores me

Sheep generally look very docile and harmless. No one thinks twice about walking through a field of sheep, but if the field had a bull in it, we would look for another route. But most shepherds would agree that under the appearance of innocence there is a stubborn streak of self-will in the sheep. It is this characteristic that David also saw in his own heart; he knew of this tendency to wander away from God and to be drawn back into sin. On many occasions he mentions this and deeply grieves over it, but also at the same time he is able to rejoice that his divine Shepherd never leaves him and always restores his soul.

Jesus tells us in Luke 15 of a shepherd who lost one of his sheep. He did not rest until he found the erring animal, and when he found it there was great joy as he restored the lost sheep to the fold. David knew that he often behaved like a wandering sheep. He says, 'I have strayed like a lost sheep' (Psalm 119:176), and in the same verse he cries out to God to seek him. If there is a tendency in sheep to wander, fortunately a good shepherd has an even greater tendency to go looking for his wayward charge.

David recognizes in himself this sheep-like characteristic and does not seek to cover it up. To hide the sin is only to delay the remedy, and to spurn the hand of grace and love of our shepherd, who longs to bring us back to himself. Robert Robinson wrote, 'Prone to wander, Lord I feel it, Prone to leave the God I love', and every Christian has to sadly agree that this is true of him also. It does not matter if we have been converted a few months or forty years, there is this proneness in our nature. The picture is not of an unregenerate person, dead in sin, but that of a saved man or woman. It is the picture of a backsliding soul, one who knows the Lord but allows his eye to wander in other directions than that which the Lord wants him to go. Both in Psalm 23 and Psalm 119 David testifies to the faithfulness of God in restoring us from the consequences of our stupid and wilful rebellions.

Backsliding

Backsliding is an insidious and cunning sin. No Christian wakes up in the morning and says, today I will backslide. Very often we are well down the path before we even realize we are on it. Backsliding starts in the heart and mind long before it reaches our feet, eyes or tongue. It may be that you never stop going to church. The outward form of religion is still in place but the heart is backslidden. It does not necessarily mean that you get drunk every Saturday night, it means that your heart is not right with God. You do not have to be very old to backslide, and you never get to the stage where you are too old for this sin. It is part and parcel of the spiritual battle every believer is in.

The backslider is one who has become weary of the fold of God. He has lost his relish for the green pastures, and the pleasures of the world prove to be more attractive to him than the things of God. No longer is his eye fixed unwaveringly upon the Shepherd. That is backsliding. Before our feet go in the path of sin, our eyes have already feasted there. The grass appears greener in another field, and stealthily or boldly the sheep leaves the fold. Very often it is a subtle thing. We just stop praying for a few weeks or neglect our Bible readings. We cut out the prayer meeting occasionally, or on a cold Sunday morning stay in bed until it is too late to go to church. That is the beginning of backsliding.

When at first you go down this path, you enjoy it so much that you wish you had gone sooner. You feel a new freedom. There is no Scripture or preaching to disturb your conscience, and by not attending church so regularly there is more time for other things. You feel free but the joys of backsliding do not last long. Sooner or later the darkness gets blacker and the backslidden Christian realizes he is in the wrong. He is out of fellowship with his Saviour and his peace has gone.

What does a Christian do when he realizes he is in a backslidden condition? He knows he ought to return to the Shepherd, but he has lost his way and the return is hard. He has drifted away from Christian friends. The Lord's day has become a bind. He has not prayed for ages and the Bible has become a boring book. His sense of sin has become deadened and his conscience hardened. To a man in such a condition restoration to his Lord and Saviour will appear to be impossible, and it would be impossible if it entirely depended upon him. But David encourages us by telling us that the Shepherd does the restoring.

The Restorer

The Good Shepherd loves his sheep and even their backsliding does not lessen that love. The Shepherd has pledged himself to allow none of his sheep to perish. He is committed to carry every last one of them safely to heaven. He says in John 17 that they belong to God, and God has given them to him so that he might give them eternal life. He is not going to lose them, and with tender love he follows them in their wanderings, and his eye is on them as much in the wilderness as it is in the fold.

Some of the most remarkable passages in Scripture are those in which we read of God's yearnings over his backslidden people. '"Return, faithless Israel", declares the Lord, "I will frown on you no longer, for I am merciful", declares the Lord, "I will not be angry for ever . . . Return, faithless people', declares the Lord, "for I am your husband"' (Jeremiah 3:12,14).

Hosea was a man called by God to live out his message. He was commanded to marry the prostitute Gomer so that he could be a picture of God's love for his prostitute people. 'Return, O Israel, to the Lord your God. Your sins have been your downfall! . . . I will heal their waywardness and love them freely, for my anger has turned away from them' (Hosea 14:1-4).

With such a God as this, why should a Christian ever need restoring? How could a believer ever wander from the Lord, whose heart is so full of love for him? The fact that a Christian does backslide shows clearly the vileness and power of sin. That someone who has tasted the grace and love of God in Christ, and known the joy of the Lord in his heart, could ever turn away from God and go back willingly into sin is almost unbelievable. Let us be clear, we are not talking about falling from grace and losing one's salvation. Thank God, that is impossible, but we are talking of a regenerate soul backslidden and in the grip of sin. There is no greater testimony than this to the power of sin, but at the same time there is no greater testimony to the love of God than that he should be willing to have such a person back. If people treated us in the same way some Christians treat God we would never bother with them again. We would say, enough is enough. But God is not like us—he restores my soul.

Why does God allow us to backslide?

If God prevented us from backsliding in the first place, there would be no need to restore us, so why does he not do that? For instance, why didn't God stop David committing adultery with Bathsheba? God is sovereign and could easily have done this. David was sleeping, and when he awoke he saw this beautiful woman bathing. The look led to the lust, and the lust led to the adultery. All God had to do was to keep David sleeping until Bathsheba had finished washing, and everything would have been all right.

We often think like that, even if we never actually say it. Such thinking shifts the blame for our sin from us to God, and it forgets that the Lord wants us to obey him because we love him and love his ways. He states his laws clearly and makes it known that he wants us to keep them. The only way to keep the law of God properly is by loving God, otherwise we are in danger of Pharisaism. The Pharisee kept the law of God, he actually did tithe and fast and pray etc., but it was a rigid legalism. God wants us to keep his laws not out of fear or legalism but because we love him and love his commandments. So he does not prevent backsliding by use of his sovereign power. He saves us by exercising this power, and we could not have been saved if he had not done so. But once saved the redeemed soul is a free soul. In sin there is no freedom. Free-will is a myth. The sinner is not free but bound by his sin. Redemption sets us free, and God wants us to exercise this freedom by pleasing him as we keep his commandments. God shows us his law and says this is what I want you to do, and if you do not do it there will be consequences to face. But he expects us to keep these commands because we love him and not because he forces us to. He wants us to love him with a heart that is free, and when we sometimes fail, he demonstrates the greatness of his love by bringing us back and restoring us. Christians wander from God because in this world we are not totally free from the pull of sin. Salvation does not prevent sin, but it does deal with the guilt of sin. There is forgiveness from our Shepherd and he will restore us. Because of his sin a Christian can lose the joy of his salvation, he can lose the sense of the presence of the Lord, but he cannot lose his salvation. If ever a man could have lost his salvation because of sin, it was David. But David knew of the restoring grace of God, and this did not cause him to trifle with sin, but to hate it even more and love his Saviour with a greater passion.

God allows his people to go so far in their rebellion, and then begins to deal with them to bring them back. He will allow problems to invade their lives. It may be illness or some other calamity, but the purpose is to show them their need of him. You see this time and time again in the history of Israel, and the same is true in the life of every believer. He may allow us to taste sin and feel its consequence, but all the time he is working to restore us, and this involves not just love on his part but also repentance from us.

Repentance

It is possible for a Christian to be found out in his sin and feel sorry for himself. He is not sorry for the sin, but sorry that he has been found out. That is not repentance. Repentance means that, even if we are not found out and if no one else knows about it, God knows and we are grieved because we have sinned against this holy God. The Lord works restoration by causing the Christian to hate the sin he has been enjoying. When David sinned against Bathsheba, he sinned against her and against her husband Uriah, but he cries out in Psalm 51, 'Against you, you only, have I sinned, and done this evil in your sight' (v.4). He realized that ultimately all sin is against God. This is why it is nonsense to excuse our sin by pleading that it does no harm to anyone. What about God? Sin grieves the Lord, and there will be no restoration until we realize this and ask for pardon. It is the Shepherd who restores, but it is on the grounds of our repentance and the longing to be right again with God.

The Prodigal Son longed to be free from the pigsty and be back in his father's house. He would have been happy to be treated as a servant and work in the kitchen, as long as he was back with the father. This is the longing that God seeks to create in the heart of the backslider. It is God who causes the longing as the backslider is aroused by the Holy Spirit. The sense of his own sin deepens. He remembers the Bible and goes back to it, perhaps in fear and uncertainty. He remembers the place of prayer and starts again haltingly to call upon God. The whole process that took him away from God is reversed by God, and even as Satan originally enticed him away, so now the Lord entices him back. There is an amazing statement in Hosea 2:14 where God talks about alluring the backsliders back to himself. He woos them, courts them and shows love to bring them back.

We ought to praise God for such love and patience. If God were to treat us as we treat him, there would be no hope for anyone. But God always loves his people. He is always alluring and wooing, always working to restore our backslidden souls. Thank God for his love, but never abuse it. Never take it for granted. If your soul needs restoring, then cry to the Shepherd who alone can do the restoring, and come to him in his prescribed way of repentance and faith.

7
He guides me

The way of restoration is always the way of repentance, and it should also result in a determination in the Christian never again to need restoring. God's way is clearly the best and no believer would argue with that, but the Christian who has made a mess of his spiritual life knows from his own experience what a fool he was to ignore the ways of God. When a soul is restored, it is restored not only back to a place of fellowship with God but also back to a place of righteousness. The soul is restored not only to happiness but also to holiness, not only to peace but also to obedience, and so David goes on to declare that the proof of the reality of this restoration is the experience of God now leading us in paths of righteousness. Why did we need restoration in the first place? It was because we had forsaken the paths of righteousness and gone down the alleys of sin. Restoration puts us back to the place we should never have left. The backsliding Christian had rejected the Shepherd's leading and gone his own way. He was indifferent to God's will and purpose in his life, but the proof of restoration is that he now values these again and wants to be led by God.

Knowing the guidance of God

This is the second time in the Psalm David has spoken of

being led by the Shepherd. He spoke firstly of God leading beside the quiet waters, that is a picture of a Christian going on with God and being led by the Holy Spirit. But sin deceived, and the quiet waters and green pastures were ignored, so he needed restoring. The proof of this is that he is being led again and he is particularly conscious that he needs to be led into and kept in the paths of righteousness.

The guidance of God is a continual necessity for the Christian. There is not a single step we can safely take heavenward unless we are led by God. The moment we become Christians our life needs to be under the continual guidance of God. Whether we are strong in faith or weak we need this divine leading, and to a great degree whether we are spiritually strong or weak will depend upon how diligent we are in following the lead given to us. We will never reach a point in our spiritual pilgrimage when our past rich experiences or our present knowledge will render it unnecessary to be led by God. Jeremiah 10:23 reminds us of this, 'I know, O Lord, that a man's life is not his own; it is not for man to direct his steps.' We do not have the ability in ourselves to direct our own steps; even the holiest believer is not equipped to safely go his own way.

We need guidance through the mine-field of this world, and David testifies that all the blessings he enjoyed were due to God's guidance. As Christians we are able to enjoy the green pastures of Scripture. It was not always like that. Our eyes and mind could see nothing in God's book of relevance or interest. Salvation changed that, but even when saved the Bible was not easy to understand. Over the years God has led us by his Holy Spirit to appreciate more and more the worth of Scripture. Doctrines which once baffled us now delight us. What appeared to be dark passages that offended

our understanding, we have now been led to love and trea-
sure. It is not just years of experience or mental astuteness
that has changed things, but the guidance and enlighten-
ment given by our Shepherd.

God is always guiding his people. This is a basic principle
of Scripture, yet somehow as Christians we have managed
to make this glorious fact into one of the most difficult and
complicated problems in the Christian life. We always seem
to have trouble on the question of guidance. How can I be
sure if God is guiding me to do a certain thing? One of the
main causes of the problem is that we seem to limit divine
guidance to the special events in life—what job to take,
whom to marry, where to live, which church to attend? The
ordinary things of every day life we feel confident in dealing with without God's help. This has got to be a fatal mistake, because God is concerned about our whole life, and his
guidance is for every situation. It is not occasional but daily,
and if we are not aware of God's daily involvement in our
lives, no wonder we struggle with respect to the special
thing. If we get to know God's guidance in the little things,
the big things will not be so much trouble. In other words, it
is a matter of living in continual communion with the Shepherd.

Have you noticed how rarely in Scripture God's people
had trouble with guidance? Abraham, Moses, David and
others may on occasions have fought against the way the
Lord was leading them, but they knew the way. The reason
for this is told us by Jesus in John 10, 'his sheep follow him
because they know his voice.' To know his voice we have to
live close to him, and when we do, guidance will not be the
major problem we have made it. Our problem is not really
one of guidance, it is one of closeness to God. Have you ever

picked up the telephone and heard the voice at the other end say, Hello, it's me. You have no idea who me is but the voice goes on, don't you recognize my voice? You are baffled because you don't recognize the voice and the reason is very simple, you have not seen this person for over ten years. Years ago when he was living next door or working with you, you would have recognized the voice instantly, but now after years of being apart you have forgotten the voice. The lesson is obvious, if you want to recognize the voice of God, stay in touch with him.

Guidance is not only a matter of a verse of Scripture apparently speaking to a situation you are in. God does speak to us through his Word, it presents us with examples and warnings, but don't make the Bible a kind of lucky dip. Guidance is much more a matter of living in the Scriptures day by day and thus getting to know the mind of God. It is communion with God in prayer and Scripture. This is how we learn to know the Shepherd's voice. There are other voices seeking to lead us astray and sometimes they quote Scripture (see Matthew 4:6 for an example). We are to be wise not gullible.

Righteousness

When God leads us he always leads in paths of righteousness. This means that if I am going God's way I will find my life being drawn closer to God. Personal holiness and sanctification will become my longing. My sense of sin will be heightened and my spiritual life deepened. God always leads this way. Whatever the circumstances, whatever the decision that has to be taken, if God is in it, it will promote righteousness in my soul and if it does not then God is not leading that way.

The Christian faith is always the way of righteousness. Whatever may be the inconsistencies of those who call themselves Christian, it is obvious that the principles of biblical faith rest on the righteousness which is the essence of God's holy character. It has no sympathy with sin, no place for deviousness and no room for worldliness. Psalm 97:2 declares that righteousness and justice are the foundations of God's throne. Proverbs 8:20 encourages us to walk in the ways of righteousness, and in the New Testament Jesus is called the Righteous One (1 John 2:1)

Jesus, our Good Shepherd, walked this path of righteousness, and of no other religious leader can it be said that his teaching and living always perfectly harmonized. Jesus is the one exception. The life he lived was in fulfilment of the law of God. His motive in everything was love for God and love for people, and this prompted all his thoughts, words and actions. The path of righteousness was Christ's natural environment and therefore he leads his sheep this way. But if righteousness is natural to Christ, it is alien to man. Both Old and New Testament declare that, 'there is no-one righteous, not even one' (Psalm 14:3 and Romans 3:10). If we are to be righteous, then we have to be made righteous, and this is the prime function of the gospel.

The righteousness we need is not a matter of our own honesty, integrity and moral character, but God's righteousness. In Philippians 3:9 Paul writes of being found in Christ, 'not having a righteousness of my own that comes from the law, but that which is through faith in Christ—the righteousness that comes from God and is by faith.' If you read the previous verses (4-6) you will see that at one time Paul had trusted a great deal in his own righteousness. But now that he was a Christian, he realized that all that was rubbish (v.8) compared to the righteousness that God provides for us.

When we became Christians, God clothed us in the righteousness of Jesus (Romans 3:21-22; 5:17; 10:3-11). This is
known as imputed or credited righteousness (Romans 4:18-
25). We are saved on the basis of Christ's righteousness being
given to us, but that is not the end of the story. There is also
imparted righteousness. Having been saved by grace and
covered with the imputed righteousness of Christ, the Holy
Spirit now begins to work within us to change and sanctify
us. Gradually our thinking, our desires and our outlook on
life begin to change. We will never be sinless in this world,
but we find ourselves hating our own sin. What happens is
that the righteousness which in our salvation was not ours,
but covered us like a robe, is now becoming part of us. We
begin to grow in grace and love for God. It is this that David
means by the paths of righteousness.

Longings

One of the evidences that a man is a Christian is that he
longs to walk in the paths of righteousness because he
knows that this is God's will for him. If we are following
the Shepherd this is the way we will be led. But it is not an
easy path; Jesus calls it narrow and the believer will stumble
sometimes or even wander off it. Progress may seem slow
on this path and the true child of God will mourn and weep
over his lack of growth in righteousness, but he keeps going. The longing for God's path is expressed several times
in the Psalms, 'My steps have held to your paths; my feet
have not slipped' (17:5); 'Send forth your light and your truth,
let them guide me' (43:3); 'Show me the way I should go,
for to you I lift up my soul' (143:8). David goes on in verse

10 to pray, 'Teach me to do your will, for you are my God; may your good Spirit lead me on level ground.'

Every Christian should have such a longing, for really it is a longing for a Christ-like life. The believer wants this because this alone will guarantee that he will be neither ineffective nor unproductive in his work for God. The path of righteousness is described in such verses as Philippians 4:8, 'Finally, brothers, whatever is true, whatever is noble, whatever is right, whatever is pure, whatever is lovely, whatever is admirable—if anything is excellent or praiseworthy—think about such things.' We see it again in 2 Peter 1:5-8, 'For this very reason, make every effort to add to your faith goodness; and to goodness, knowledge; and to knowledge, self-control; and to self-control, perseverance; and to perseverance, godliness; and to godliness, brotherly kindness; and to brotherly kindness, love. For if you possess these qualities in increasing measure, they will keep you from being ineffective and unproductive in your knowledge of our Lord Jesus Christ.'

God is concerned to see holiness in his people and we too should share this concern. If the longing is in us, then we should follow Peter's advice and make every effort to see that, when the Shepherd leads us to the paths of righteousness, we stay there and seek to cultivate in our lives the graces that please God, and so enrich us. Without the longing for holiness we will not know the reality of it. The longing will ensure that we follow where the Shepherd leads and that the aura of righteousness will not be repugnant to us or restrictive but the thing that we delight in above all else. The world hates righteousness, it mocks it and calls it weakness. It cannot stand it because it cannot understand it. But the Christian longs for it and knows that there is no substitute for righteousness in his life.

His name's sake

As we look around us we see a world that is sick. Vice des-
troys virtue, the wicked prosper and the good suffer, the
light of the gospel is hated and the darkness of sin is loved.
But even worse than that, we see sin in our own hearts. We
who are Christians, regenerate and indwelt by the Holy
Spirit, still seem unable to deal with sin. In the light of this
we wonder if righteousness ever can reign? Why does God
even bother with us? It is certainly not because we deserve
anything, it is for his name's sake.

In Ezekiel 36 God is dealing with rebellious Israel. Once
again they have forsaken the Lord and gone off to idols, but
God shows mercy to them and says in verse 22, 'It is not for
your sake, O house of Israel, that I am going to do these
things, but for the sake of my holy name, which you have
profaned among the nations where you have gone.' Our sin
as Christians brings dishonour upon the name of God, but he
restores us because the Lord is concerned with the glory and
holiness of his name. In 1 Samuel 12, the Lord is dealing with
the same problem, and Samuel declares in verse 22, 'For the
sake of his great name the Lord will not reject his people,
because the Lord was pleased to make you his own.'

'His name's sake' reminds us that all God's dealings with
us are on the basis of his free unmerited grace and not because
of anything we think we deserve. We may be wayward
sheep but he will always be the Good Shepherd. He has
pledged himself to lose none of his sheep. It is true that he
loves us and he is a God full of mercy, but ultimately the prime
motive for all that God does is his own name, honour and
glory. This truth alone can give us comfort amidst all the
struggles of life and encourage us under the burden of our
own sinfulness. Despite all our failings we shall not be cast

out by God; we shall not lose our salvation. God's glory is wrapped up in our salvation because he himself has made it so. We know what our sin deserves, but we rejoice when we read verses like Isaiah 48:9-11, 'For my own name's sake I will delay my wrath; for the sake of my praise I hold it back from you, so as not to cut you off. See, I have refined you, though not as silver; I have tested you in the furnace of affliction. For my own sake, for my own sake, I do this. How can I let myself be defamed? I will not yield my glory to another.'

Why does God bother with us? Because he loves us? Yes praise God that is true, but he also loves us because of the glory of his own name. On this ground we approach God for forgiveness. Like David we pray, 'For the sake of your name, O Lord, forgive my iniquity though it is great' (Psalm 25:11). Another Psalmist, Asaph, does the same thing, 'Help us, O God our Saviour, for the glory of your name; deliver us and atone for our sins for your name's sake' (79:9). These men knew how to approach God. What a joy to hear the answer of Isaiah 43:25, 'I, even I, am he who blots out your transgressions, for my own sake, and remembers your sins no more.'

This is how God loves us and this is how we are to approach God when we feel guilty and sinful. We deserve nothing. We may be bad sheep but the Lord is always the Good Shepherd.

8

He removes my
fear of death

There are many people who play at Christianity. They are one thing in church on a Sunday, and something totally different for the rest of the week at home or at work. No one could accuse David of that. There were times when he sinned and failed in his submission to God, but to him the Lord was always the most important person, and his faith was both serious and real. If someone were to ask David, how far are you prepared to go in your trust of God? His answer would be, I will trust him even into the valley of the shadow of death.

David's spirit has been lifted up by reviewing the way that God has dealt graciously with him. It is good for us as Christians to follow this example. As we think about God's mercy, patience, love and all the blessings that flow from these, we too will find our hearts elated. This is not merely a subjective emotional experience but a delighting in the reality of being led by the Shepherd. David was experiencing a deep awareness of past and present mercies, and this produced a persuasion of the Lord's unchanging love for him right through his life and even through death. Here is a faith for the future based on the fact and experience of what God has already done for us.

The valley

The phrase 'the valley of the shadow of death' is one peculiar to Scripture and ancient Near-Eastern literature. It is used to represent those terrible trials and extreme difficulties which no man or woman can completely avoid in this life. There can be little doubt that in the Psalm David thinks beyond these to death itself, that last enemy—the ultimate danger. He compares dying to a deep valley, dark and gloomy and full of frightening shadows. He must go through this valley because there is no bypass to it. We all know this for we have seen loved ones and friends go this way. It does not matter what we are in life, rich or poor, young or old, healthy or sickly, all came eventually to this valley. Every person has to face death so this is very real for us all.

Unlike today's attitude to this awful reality here is a picture of death not coloured by sentiment. We live in what has been called a permissive society where things are supposedly openly talked about and faced up to. This is so true in certain areas like sex but in our attitude to death we are more suppressed today than many past generations. Sentiment and evasion dominate most people's attitude to death. If an old person dies we say they have had a long life so their death is to be expected, but if a teenager dies we see that as a tragedy. That is only sentiment because we fail to ask if the person was ready to face death and we totally ignore God in our thinking. This is because God is a stranger to most people and therefore our only shield against the inevitability of death is sentiment and fear and superstition. So society has turned back to the ouija board and black magic, to fortune tellers and horoscopes. People are looking for answers but they will not look to God. They know the valley is there but are totally unable to cope with it.

How different was David's approach to death. He actually makes a theological statement and when we are talking about death we have to be theological, not sentimental. Death is a valley. All men prefer to live on the mountain peaks of health and happiness, but they must go down into this valley sometime. The frightening thing to man is that he has no control as to when he goes into the valley. Youngsters and old folk, men at the peak of physical fitness as well as those who have spent long months of lingering illness are suddenly called to this valley. This fact makes folly of how most people live. They like to think they are masters of their own destiny but when death calls there is no appeal, no argument and no turning back. Death is the great valley that separates this world from the next and we will all go into it.

The reality of death

What is death? Is it merely the cessation of life in this mortal body after which there is no more? Most people believe it is because it is convenient for them to do so, but the Bible teaches that death is not the end. Death is a judgment. Man was created to live not die. So why does death exist? Why will we all die? When we die a doctor will write on our death certificate the cause of death. He may write heart failure, cancer or whatever it is, but that will not be the cause of death. That is simply the means by which death has come. The doctor is giving a physical reason only for death, but God in his Word declares that the reason is not physical but theological. Death is the wages of sin. We die because we are all sinners.

Loraine Boettner in his book *Immortality*, tells us that the Bible speaks of death in three ways. Spiritual death is the separation of the soul from God. This is the condition all men and women are in because of their sin. Physical death is the separation of the soul from the body. This is what is generally known as death and is also part of the penalty for sin. Eternal death is spiritual death made permanent.

Everyone accepts the reality of physical death but spiritual and therefore eternal death are not so readily accepted. There are several reasons for this. One is that physical death is tangible and can be seen, whereas spiritual and eternal death do not for most people have this reality. This is because God is not taken seriously in their thinking and interpretation of life. Once the fact of God is rejected then all that matters is the here and now. Present happiness, prosperity and materialism becomes a reasonable philosophy and death is only a cessation of life with nothing after it. Therefore there is nothing to fear in death and in certain circumstances it may even be welcomed. But most people do fear death. When David says that in the experience of death he will fear no evil, he says so because this is unusual and most folk are terrified of death. Atheists, agnostics, rejecters of God, fear death. But why is this if death is only the end of physical life? Is it that such people's beliefs are not strong enough to cope with the reality of death? Why is it that when people who never attend church die, their relatives want a vicar to stand over their coffin and bury them 'in sure and certain hope of resurrection unto life eternal'? Is it perhaps that spiritual and eternal death are not myths after all?

The fact is that death ushers sinners into the presence of the holy God. We all have to stand before the judgment seat of God and give an account for our sin. Heaven and hell await us and without a Saviour we have no hope, therefore sinners ought to fear death. They have every reason to fear it.

The reality of death means the reality of judgment and without a Saviour that means hell.

The shadow

David was a sinner so why didn't he fear death? The answer is, the Lord is my Shepherd. Jesus the Good Shepherd gave his life for the sheep. He died to pay the price of their sin, to save them, to redeem them and to make them acceptable to God. In his death he has conquered death for his people. He has destroyed death (2 Timothy 1:10) and given us the victory over it (1 Corinthians 15:54-57). But is not physical death still a reality even for Christians? Yes it is, but now it is a shadow of the real thing. A shadow is a shape cast by a real object but it is not real in and of itself. You can walk through the shadow of a tree but you cannot walk through the tree. This is what David means. Death is still there but there is no power in it for the Christian. The terror and sting has been taken away and it is merely like walking through a shadow.

The sting of death is sin and once our sin has been dealt with by the Good Shepherd there is nothing to fear in it. Charles Spurgeon preaching on Colossians 2:15 depicts the battle on the cross between Christ and Satan. In vivid and wonderful language he says, 'Satan came against Christ; he had in his hand a sharp sword called the Law, dipped in the poison of sin, so that every wound which the law inflicted was deadly. Christ dashed this sword out of Satan's hand, and there stood the prince of darkness unarmed. His helmet was cleft in twain, and his head was crushed as with a rod of iron. Death rose against Christ. The Saviour snatched his quiver from him, emptied out all his darts, cut them in two, gave Death back the feather end, but kept the poison barbs from him, that he might never destroy the ransom.' In this amazing picture Spurgeon reminds us that death has only the feathered end of his arrows to use against the Christian. With these he may irritate and disturb but he cannot harm because Christ has taken from him the poisoned barbs of destruction.

It is in the light of this truth that David is able to say that he is not afraid to walk into the valley of death. The word walk depicts an attitude of composure. He does not have to be dragged into the valley nor is he running into it in terror and panic. He walks. He is not going to hasten impatiently, neither is he going to hold back reluctantly. He walks with the step of one who is sure that he knows where he is going. He knows the valley is not an end in itself. He will walk *through* it. Through means in and out the other end. Praise God there is an exit and the exit is the house of the Lord forever. The valley of the shadow of death is to the Christian what the valley of water at the Red Sea was to Moses and the Israelites. They had come out of bondage and were on the way to the Promised Land but then Pharaoh came after them with his army to put them back into slavery. The sea was in front of them and the enemy behind. Their situation seemed impossible but then God intervened. He opened the sea and a valley was cut through the impassable waters and they walked through in safety to the other side. When Pharaoh tried to do the same thing the banked up waters came down upon him and destroyed him. The way God had provided was for the redeemed only. There was no way and hope there for the unbeliever.

Shadows can sometimes be frightening. They play tricks on our imagination and plant all sorts of unfounded fears in our minds. Death though it is only a shadow can do the same thing. Even though its sting has been removed it can still plant fears in the Christian's mind. The result is that though death is nothing to fear, dying can be a real problem. The pain, the suffering, the anguish that we may have to experience or see loved ones experience can do damage to a person's faith. For instance, I have had two heart attacks and I do not want another one, but the probability is that at some point in the future I will. And it could be that eventually a heart attack will kill me. If I am to spend the rest of my life in fear of a heart attack it will rob me of the joy and peace of salvation. If I am to let the means by which death comes to me dominate my thinking and forget that the cause of my eventual death, sin, has been dealt with once and for all by my Saviour, then I will live a life of spiritual defeat. Our joy as Christians is to know that, '"Death has been swallowed up in victory. Where, O death, is your victory? Where, O death, is your sting?" The sting of death is sin, and the power of sin is the law. But thanks be to God! He gives us the victory through our Lord Jesus Christ' (1 Corinthians 15:54-57).

For a shadow to come into being it needs two things—a real object and light. It is the light shining on the object that casts the shadow. Death is the real object, dark and frightening, but if the light of God shines on it, it will cast a shadow and it is that shadow of death that the Christian will have to face. Even then he will not have to face it alone because the Shepherd will be with him.

9
He comforts me

Psalm 23 is not a prayer. It is not something David wants to happen in his life but what he has already known and experienced of God. That being the case we will be making a major mistake if we do as most unbelievers do with this Psalm and sentimentalize it. To be lost in its beauty can make us miss the reality of David's experience. We need to know God as the Psalmist did.

Because God's presence was so real to David, he also knew when God was not with him. In other Psalms we find this man crying to the Lord to come to him or not to leave him. God's nearness was important to David. It was not blessings he wanted but God himself. The best and holiest men of any generation have earnestly prayed for the enjoyment of God's presence as the very strength of their heart, the foundation of their joy and the centre of their existence. Moses trembled at the thought of God leaving him, 'If your Presence does not go with us, do not send us up from here' (Exodus 33:15), he said. In the shipwreck in Acts 27 everyone was panicking except Paul. The secret of the Apostle's peace was his awareness of the nearness of God amidst all the confusion. The same man with his friend Silas in Acts 16 could sing hymns while his back was bleeding and his feet fast in the stocks in the jail at Philippi. They knew God was with them and the comfort that came from such knowledge overshadowed even their awful predicament.

Reality

David in the Psalm says, I will fear no evil, not because I am brave, but because you are with me. This was his comfort and it is not something we need only when facing death but at all times. If God is real to us in life he will also be real in death. The reality of God with us will make a difference to the sort of Christian we will be in our daily work. It will affect how we cope with life's trials and tribulations. Victorious Christian living is living in the presence of God. That is where our strength comes from. So often we tremble before the pygmies of the world because we try to succeed in our own strength, but when like David we can say, you are with me, we will defeat even the Goliaths. All the giants of the world are no match for a Christian standing in the power of God.

Jesus said that without him we could do nothing. That is a strong claim but we know from experience that it is perfectly true, and it is also true that we can do all things through Christ who strengthens us. The early Christians in the New Testament were only very ordinary men and women but they turned the world upside-down. This was not done by political power or organized labour but by the spiritual strength of the indwelling Holy Spirit. The marvellous promise of Isaiah 43:2-3,5 should be our experience daily, 'When you pass through the waters, I will be with you; and when you pass through the rivers, they will not sweep over you. When you walk through the fire, you will not be burnt; the flames will not set you ablaze. For I am the Lord, your

God, the Holy One of Israel, your Saviour . . . do not be afraid, for I am with you.'

If these words from Isaiah are not real to us, it is because sin has blotted out the reality of the divine presence and we are left cold and miserable. God's presence is still there but our sin has blocked out the reality of it and we are unable to feel and appreciate it. It is like sitting on a beach on a hot summer day enjoying the sun. It is pleasant and peaceful but suddenly you feel cold and uncomfortable. The reason is that a cloud has blotted out the sun from you and you do not feel its heat and comfort. The sun is still shining and you know that in your mind but in your experience it is as if it is not there.

Knowing and believing that the sun is shining behind the cloud does not warm you. You need to feel it but you will not do so until the cloud moves away. Sin in our lives acts like the cloud. We will not enjoy the reality of God's presence whilst we harbour sin in our lives. Deal with the sin and the sun will shine again.

The great words of Isaiah 43 will not comfort us unless we know and experience the reality of them. The great men of Scripture were not satisfied in knowing that the Lord was near. They wanted to feel and experience the reality of his nearness. This is particularly important when we have to face death. John Wesley could say of the first Methodists, 'our people die well.' This was true not only because they believed what the Scripture said about death, but also because the God who had been with them in life was also with them in the dark valley. That was their comfort. Vavasor Powell, the Welsh Puritan, said, 'The fear of death is engrafted in the common nature of all men, but faith works it out of Christians.' Faith works this terrible fear out of the

Christian both by the objective truth of Scripture and the subjective experience of God's presence.

Rod and staff

David had more than his fair share of problems in life. Some were of his own making and others the result of attacks by his enemies. Comfort from God was something he was continually in need of, and he says that he got this comfort from the Shepherd's rod and staff.

Whether the rod and staff were two separate objects or two different uses to which the shepherd put his crook is unimportant. The comfort comes from the fact that it is the hand of the Shepherd which is using it. They make the sheep aware that the shepherd is near and the sheep know that the rod and staff are always used for the good of the flock.

The rod was used to gather the sheep together and to count them—'every tenth animal that passes under the shepherd's rod will be holy to the Lord' (Leviticus 27:32). The sheep passing under the rod signified ownership and possession. In Jeremiah 10 Israel is called the rod of God's inheritance (verse 16, AV) and in Ezekiel 20:37, 'I will take note of you as you pass under my staff (rod), and I will bring you into the bond of the covenant.' The Christian has passed under the rod of God. He has chosen us and claimed us as his own. We belong to God and there is no greater comfort than that.

The rod was also a symbol of the shepherd's power and authority. With the rod he controlled the flock. If a sheep started to wander away it would feel the rod on its back to remind it that it belonged to the shepherd and was not to go its own way. The rod was thus an instrument of correction and punishment. God says in Psalm 89:32, 'I will punish their sin with the rod.' Paul uses the same language in writing to the Corinthians, 'shall I come unto you with a rod or in love' (1 Corinthians 4:21,AV). The Apostle was having trouble with the church at Corinth and threatens to come to them with a rod of discipline. The NIV says 'with a whip.' Strange as it may seem, there is always in God's ministry of discipline upon us a great element of comfort, for it is those whom he loves that he disciplines. When God punishes us because of our sin it is a proof of his displeasure but at the same time it reminds us of his love and nearness.

The rod was used to protect the sheep as wolves and lions would be fended off with it. David uses this idea in Psalm 2:8-9 when talking about God blessing his people, 'Ask of me, and I will make the nations your inheritance, and the ends of the earth your possession. You will break them with a rod of iron [NIV margin].'

The staff was really a rod with a hook on the end and was used to deliver the sheep from trouble and dangerous situations. The shepherd would hook it around a sheep that had fallen into some danger and pull it back to safety. Our Good Shepherd is forever exercising his love and grace to deliver us from evil. We would not last five minutes in this world on our own, but thank God our Shepherd is always near us.

The rod and staff are nothing without the hand of the Shepherd to use and direct them and comfort comes not from them but from him. In our trials and in the stresses of life we may be tempted to think that our greatest comfort would come if we had better health or a better job and more money. That is to trust in the rod and staff, not the Shepherd. Real comfort comes from an awareness of the love and grace of the Good Shepherd. In a world sick with sin the Christian is always in need of comfort. Isaiah 40 starts with the words, 'Comfort, comfort my people, says your God.' The people of God at that time had forgotten certain things. Forgetfulness at times can be a little awkward, even embarrassing, but if as believers we forget what these folk had forgotten we are in serious trouble. They had forgotten who their God was and what he was capable of doing. Twice in verse 21 and 28 the prophet has to ask them, 'Do you not know? Have you not heard?' The reason for this disastrous lapse was that they were overwhelmed by circumstances that led them to conclude that the Lord was no longer interested in them (verse 27). The result was that they wallowed in self-pity. They were weary, tired, stumbling and falling. God deals with this by bringing them the comfort of a fresh vision of the greatness, love and power that he exercises on their behalf. At the beginning of a thrilling description of the power of God from verse 10 onwards we are introduced yet again to the picture of God as a Shepherd. 'He tends his flock like a shepherd: He gathers the lambs in his arms and carries them close to his heart' (verse 11). There is real comfort for a believer in this truth. To say the Lord is my Shepherd is to claim that all the power and might that Isaiah describes is working for us. Our Shepherd is 'the Father of all compassion and the God of all comfort' (2 Corinthians 1:3) and he will never forsake his sheep.

10
He prepares a table for me

Sheep have many enemies. Most wild animals find sheep an easy prey and there are also thieves whose only desire towards the helpless animal is, as Jesus said in John 10, to steal and kill and destroy. Even the people hired to look after the sheep have no love for them; at the first sign of trouble they leave the sheep to their own devices. So the sheep is a very vulnerable animal. The only one who really has its welfare in mind is the shepherd. If for a moment the shepherd relaxes his vigilance the sheep's enemies will attack and destroy. They are never far away and they are always looking for an opportunity to strike, but fortunately for the sheep the shepherd is permanently nearby to protect and care for his beloved flock.

David took great comfort from this. He too had many enemies and was always aware of their attention. The believer is in the same position because the Christian life is a continual battle. The spiritual enemies that we have to face are all around us and the battle is very real. But even in the hottest action there are spiritual provisions for us from the table of the Lord. This table of mercy and grace is spread for us not only when things are relatively easy and comfortable but also in times of our greatest needs. The Shepherd is not restricted by the presence of enemies. When they are doing their best to destroy the sheep of God, he calmly prepares a table so that the sheep can feed and be nourished for the battle. The enemies' efforts are continually aimed at stopping the sheep feeding on the provisions of the Shepherd. All sorts of devices are used to ensure this end—fear, confusion, stubbornness. But for every scheme of the enemy the Shepherd has an answer and the sheep have only to avail themselves from that which is spread on the table for them.

The Lord God Jehovah is David's Shepherd and his King and here he sees himself as the Lord's guest, invited to feast at his banqueting table. Every true believer is a guest of God. We can only enter his presence by invitation. He calls us from darkness to light and continually through our Christian life he is the generous host providing for all our needs. Those who come are always satisfied: in Psalm 36:8 David describes the joy of being at the Lord's table, 'They feast on the abundance of your house; you give them drink from your rivers of delight.' The beautiful language of Proverbs 9:1-6 describes the Lord's gracious invitation to dine at his table, 'Wisdom has built her house; she has hewn out its seven pillars. She has prepared her meat and mixed her wine; she has also set her table. She has sent out her maids, and she calls from the highest point of the city. "Let all who are simple come in here", she says to those who lack judgment. "Come, eat my food and drink the wine I have mixed. Leave your simple ways and you will live; walk in the way of understanding."' This closely corresponds to the invitation given by Jesus at the beginning of Matthew 22, 'The kingdom of heaven is like a king who prepared a wedding banquet for his son. He sent his servants to those who had been invited to the banquet to tell them to come, but they refused to come.

Then he sent some more servants and said, "Tell those who have been invited that I have prepared my dinner: My oxen and fattened cattle have been slaughtered, and everything is ready. Come to the wedding banquet."'

Table

Table, a comprehensive term used to denote all manner of provisions which may be needful or desirable, speaks of the wonder of all that God provides for his people. As it is God himself who provides this table the supplies are always abundant. There is no menu here from which to make a selection, for all that God provides we need, and if we are in true fellowship with him what he provides will all be a delight to us. It is not for us to pick and choose, or to express our likes and dislike, but rather to accept gratefully all that the Lord provides. All we need in this life we will find at his table. It is full of all manner of blessings, every type of spiritual provision is prepared for us. No Christian can ever say, I needed grace and there was none available. Nor can any say, I needed wisdom but the cupboard was bare. Grace, wisdom, strength, and everything else needed for the Christian life are supplied by our Shepherd. We bring nothing to this table but a humble sense of our own unworthiness and a grateful sense of God's marvellous goodness and kindness. The only thing that we bring with us are a spiritual hunger and an appetite for the things of God.

There are no shortages or rationing of God's mercies. His gifts are always 'a good measure, pressed down, shaken together and running over' (Luke 6:38). God is by nature inclined to bestow blessings and he takes a holy pleasure in the happiness of his people. Thus the Psalmist says that God is good (100:5) and does good (103:5). And there is about God's goodness an infinite generosity without which we would be not only the poorer but also hopeless. He is 'the Lord, the Lord, the compassionate and gracious God, slow to anger, abounding in love and faithfulness, maintaining love to thousands, and forgiving wickedness, rebellion and sin' (Exodus 34:6-7).

The church is vast and its members unnumbered yet there is not one of the redeemed whose circumstances God is not aware of and whose needs he cannot supply. Isaiah rejoices that, 'the Lord Almighty will prepare a feast of rich food for all peoples, a banquet of aged wine—the best of meats and the finest of wines' (25:6). We should never lose sight of this glorious fact. The eternal God is committed to caring for and protecting his people. The table is prepared at all times which means that no crisis that may confront us will take God unawares. And it is prepared 'before me'—this means I do not have to go looking or wondering where the mercies of God are, they are staring me in the face and ready to be used.

Prepared

God is not a God of chance or circumstance: everything he does is planned and prepared. Our salvation was a prepared salvation, prepared in heaven before the world was created. And Jesus was the lamb slain before the foundation of the world. In fact all God's mercies are prepared mercies (Psalm 68:7-10; 1 Corinthians 2:9; Hebrews 11:13-16; John 14:2-3). When that preparation is finally complete, Jesus will return again for his people and they will hear him say, 'Come, you who are blessed by my Father; take your inheritance, the kingdom prepared for you since the creation of the world' (Matthew 25:34).

Preparation suggests that it is done carefully, lovingly and with expectation. When the Lord prepares to meet our needs only the best is good enough. Yet he expects us to draw near and eat. The Christian is to taste and see that the Lord is good; we have food to eat that the world knows nothing of and the table is spread for the here and now. When Paul in 1 Corinthians 2:9 quotes Isaiah 64, 'no eye has seen, no ear has heard, no mind has conceived what God has prepared for those who love him', he is not referring to heaven but to present blessing in this life that the believer is to look for and expect. The table is not in heaven but before us now, so the Lord in Isaiah says, 'I am bringing my righteousness near; it is not far away; and my salvation will not be delayed' (4:13). The words of Jesus to his church are, 'I stand at the door and knock. If anyone hears my voice and opens the door, I will go in and eat with him, and he with me' (Revelation 3:20).

An appetite

We will only eat at the prepared table if we have an appetite for the things of God. So often Christians spoil their spiritual appetites by eating the scraps and crumbs left over from the Devil's provision for the world. If our minds and hearts are filled with the trash of sin we will never hunger and thirst after righteousness. The table is prepared in the presence of our spiritual enemies but they do not want us to eat. The Devil knows that if our appetite is for the things of the world we will always be weak and useless Christians. It does not matter what our abilities are if our appetite is wrong, we will be wrong. So the Devil is always feeding us worldly titbits.

He dangles them before us. They look good and taste good, but spiritually they are disastrous.

We need to guard our minds because if we do not think like Christians we will never live like Christians. So Paul's advice in Philippians 4:8-9 is crucial, 'whatever is true, whatever is noble, whatever is right, whatever is pure, whatever is lovely, whatever is admirable—if anything is excellent or praiseworthy— think about such things. Whatever you have learned or received or heard from me, or seen in me—put it into practice. And the God of peace will be with you.' Dr. Lloyd-Jones comments on these verses: 'Search your Bible from beginning to end and you will find that all the promises of blessing are conditional . . . take the Beatitudes from the Sermon on the Mount; Blessed are the meek . . . Blessed are the poor in spirit and so on. These are the people who are blessed, yet, there is always the condition; you must be meek and poor in spirit; you must hunger and thirst after righteousness if you want to be filled. We are not told that we shall be filled because we are Christians, no, we have to hunger and thirst and then we shall be filled, and blessed. And now we find this great exposition of that principle in the ninth verse of this last chapter of Philippians.'

What fools we are as Christians to long for the Devil's scraps when the Lord prepares a banquet for us. Daniel and his three friends refused to defile themselves by eating at the pagan king's table. We read in Daniel 1:16, 'So the guard took away their choice food and the wine they were to drink and gave them vegetables instead.' At God's table they received wisdom, understanding and power. And their knowledge of God became more than theoretical. The three gladly trusted him in the fiery furnace and so did Daniel in the den of lions. Because their appetite was for God and they ate at the Lord's table, their experience of God was rich. The enemies were still there with their plots and schemes but these men knew great victories in the most hopeless of situations. If our appetite for the things of God is right, then rich indeed will be our experience of the blessings of God.

11
He anoints me

In biblical times to anoint someone's head with oil was a demonstration of the honour and esteem one person had for another, particularly for a guest in his home. When Jesus visited the home of Simon the Pharisee, as recorded in Luke 7, he rebuked his host for, among other things, not anointing his head with oil. Simon's reception of Jesus, wrote William Hendriksen, 'had been cold, patronizing and discourteous.' David sees God's reception of him as the exact opposite of this. 'You anoint my head with oil' speaks of the honour and esteem that God bestows on all his people as they come to him. We forget sometimes how rich we are as Christians. We can be great complainers and overlook the mercies and blessings which the Lord daily loads us with. David here enters deeply into the mind and purpose of God; he goes beyond feeling a sense of inadequacy, as a sheep depending upon the Shepherd, to seeing his privilege of feeding at the table of the Lord and being received as a friend. He is still aware of his own weakness and knows he needs to be provided for and led and restored, but now there is also the awareness of the glory God has chosen to pour upon him as a redeemed sinner.

Here is a major lesson for all believers. The Christian should always have these two convictions at all times. He is safe and strong when he is aware both of his own great need and of his supreme privilege.

Balance

A lack of balance can be a serious problem for a Christian. On the one hand we need to have a conviction of our own unworthiness. We must never lose sight of the fact that we are sinners, sheep who have gone astray and need restoring. This stirs up a greater awareness of our indebtedness to God and should lead to a greater devotion and earnestness in our Christian life. On the other hand, we need to remember that we are the recipients of God's favour and blessing. He has anointed us, received us with joy and regards us as a special people. This awareness will animate our souls to greater urgency in things like prayer and holiness and meditation.

Both a sense of our own unworthiness and an awareness that we are recipients of God's favour are essential for a healthy Christian life. The believer who does not cultivate self-examination will soon relax his vigilance, soon become proud, arrogant and prayerless. Yet the believer who forgets that there is more to the Christian life than just self-examination will soon lose heart, become dejected, depressed and miserable. His only thought will be of how great a failure he is in the Christian life.

The Psalmist is balanced. He knows he is unworthy but at the same time he is able to delight that God anoints his head with oil. David was a lost sheep and trembled at the sense of his own weakness, but his thinking did not stop there. He did not allow his sense of unworthiness to cause him to doubt the mercies and blessings of divine grace. The Devil is happy to see lop-sided Christians, that is believers who are ever lamenting over their own failures but do not seem able to see and appreciate God's goodness. We are all failures to some degree and we certainly all sin, but if we are saved then we are the Lord's people and we have the anointing with the oil of God's Spirit. This does not make us complacent and indifferent to our sin but it will keep us balanced and going forward. We can lose a great deal of the joy of salvation through this lack of balance and then everything in the Christian life becomes a burden.

If we are not balanced we will fall flat on our faces, and it does not matter in which direction the unbalance lies the end result will be the same. For instance, it is possible to be too enthusiastic as Christians. That may sound strange: most believers probably are not enthusiastic enough! But enthusiasm is not enough. Zeal is not enough. The balanced life will have these but other things as well. It is only the balanced man who can walk straight. A young baby may have plenty of energy and make a great deal of noise but it cannot walk until it learns balance. When a baby starts to walk it wobbles all over the place. But when the balance comes then the wobbling stops and the child can go forward straight and with confidence. As Christians we are not to be babes in our appetites nor in our walking. A sense of balance is essential and this will involve both an awareness of our sin and also an awareness of our privilege as believers.

Honoured

It is right and proper that we honour God because he deserves all the honour we could possibly bestow upon him. But God also honours us. We can deserve nothing of this but none the less he reminds us in Isaiah 43:4, 'you are precious and honoured in my sight.' All the redeemed are precious to God. He loves and honours them. There are fellow believers of whom we may not think very highly, but God honours them. He does not write off Christians the way we do. He honours his people and he demonstrates this by anointing their heads with oil.

Oil is one of the biblical symbols for the Holy Spirit. There are many other symbols like fire, wind, the dove etc., but oil is one of the most significant of these pictures or emblems. In the Old Testament oil was used in most religious services instigated by God and was a vivid symbol of the presence of the Holy Spirit among the people. Oil penetrates. Oil softens. Oil heals. Oil strengthens. Oil preserves. According to the way it is used in Scripture oil can consecrate, can beautify, can illuminate. All these things teach us of the power and work of God the Holy Spirit. The anointing of the Holy Spirit upon the believer penetrates his soul like oil. Nothing gets through to a man like the Holy Spirit. The words of a preacher can penetrate the mind of a man and may even touch his heart, but it is only as these words are taken by the Spirit that they will penetrate both the heart and soul. Oil softens the hard heart and makes it pliable and receptive. This is the ministry of the Holy Spirit. He also heals our spiritual wounds, illuminates our dark understanding, strengthens and preserves our godly resolutions. It is the Spirit who consecrates the believer for Christ's service, who fills the saint with joy and who adorns him with holiness. The anointing with oil is a picture of all this in the Christian life.

In the Old Testament every priest and every vessel used in the service of God was anointed with oil. This symbolized that they were being set aside for the service of God. David himself was anointed with oil by Samuel when he was set apart as God's chosen king. In the New Testament this changes, and the change starts with Jesus. He was anointed not with oil but directly by the Holy Spirit at his baptism. As oil was poured upon Aaron as the first High Priest and on every High Priest who followed him, so the Holy Spirit was poured upon Jesus symbolising that he was set apart to be the Great High Priest of God's people. So Jesus was the Messiah (a Hebrew word), he was the Christ (a Greek word), and both titles mean that he was the Anointed One.

The followers of the Lord Jesus Christ are called Christians, which means that they too are anointed. The oil of spiritual anointing which was poured upon our Saviour is poured upon his Church as well. He is the anointed head of the Church and we as the body of Christ also have this anointing of the Holy Spirit. And, says Paul, if we do not have it then we do not belong to Christ. All Christians are anointed men and women. We are saved but we are also precious to God and honoured in his sight.

Anointed

Peter describes our honour and privilege as Christians in 1 Peter 2:9-10, 'But you are a chosen people, a royal priesthood, a holy nation, a people belonging to God, that you may declare the praises of him who called you out of darkness into his wonderful light. Once you were not a people, but now you are the people of God; once you had not received mercy, but now you have received mercy.'

There is a vast difference between Christ's anointing and ours but these words of Peter ooze with the sense of the honour and privilege that comes to the Christian in his salvation. Peter says, you are, he doesn't say you will be. These are true of us now. Of course there is so much that we need as believers. We need to be holier; we need to be filled with the Holy Spirit; we need revival in the Church. Perhaps we can be so overwhelmed by what we need that we forget what we already have. We are an anointed people and that ought to mean something in the every day business of living for the glory of God. We are not what we once were. And it is not just that we have changed our beliefs and behaviour. We are a chosen people, the people of God. To be called a Christian is a honour above all honours. When you say that you are a Christian it means you are an anointed one. The Old Testament says that the name of the Lord is like a perfume poured out. There is a sweetness and beauty about it. If that is true about the name of Christ, it ought also to be true of the name of Christian. A Christian ought to bring into this sin—sick world the aroma of Christ. Paul speaks of God spreading the fragrance of the knowledge of Christ everywhere through us (2 Corinthians 2:14).

The Spirit of God dwells within us and our business as the people of God is to live our lives according to that indwelling presence. We are not nobodies, we are God's people. It is sad to hear Christians apologizing for their beliefs and patterns of behaviour as if these are something to be ashamed of. The world will scorn and abuse you but you have more potential power than all the rulers of the world because you have access to God by prayer. So never forget who you are. You are anointed by God to live for his glory.

You may complain that you don't feel very special and seem to know so little of the Spirit's power in your life. That may be true and it could be that you are grieving or quenching the Spirit, but it does not change who you are. You need to submit to what God wants to do in and through you. If your heart is hard let the Holy Spirit come and soak it with his influences. If you feel spiritually wounded and weak let the Spirit heal the wounds. So often as believers we spend more time frustrating the purposes of God than submitting to the privilege of being used by the Holy Spirit.

If you can say the Lord is my Shepherd, then you can also say, You anoint my head with oil. If you are saved there is a power in you that was not there before, so submit to the Holy Spirit's leading and expect to see the difference in your life.

12
He causes my cup to overflow

David is still caught up with the privilege of being a sheep in the flock of God and with the blessings which the Shepherd continually pours upon him. He uses the word 'cup' in the same way that Jesus does in the Gospels when he asked James and John if they could drink of the cup he was going to drink. He was not referring to a literal cup but to the suffering he was going to endure. Cup in Scripture can be a cup of sorrow or a cup of joy. For instance in Psalm 11:6, 'Upon the wicked he will rain coals. Fire and brimstone and a burning wind; *this shall be* the portion of their cup' (NKJV). Here the cup is clearly a cup of sorrow, but in Psalm 16:5 it is a cup of blessing and joy, 'Lord, you have assigned me my portion and my cup; you have made my lot secure.' In Psalm 23 David means a cup of joy as God bestows great blessing upon him—his cup overflows.

David has already made reference to the mercies of God in providing for his needs twice in the Psalm—I shall lack nothing, and you prepare a table for me, really say the same thing. This continual emphasis serves to remind us that we need to appreciate what the Lord does for us. We saw in the last chapter the need of balance in the Christian life and there is certainly a need for this as we evaluate the circumstances that confront us every day. It is so easy to be absorbed in the problems and forget the blessings. The quaint old Cornish preacher Billy Bray once rebuked his congregation for having less sense than his ducks. He said that when he fed the ducks they did not pick up the rubbish and leave the grain: rather they ignored what was bad for them and enjoyed the good provision. We all have our share of problems, but if David is correct we also have more than our fair share of blessings. The hymn writer tells us to count our blessings and it will surprise us what the Lord has done.

Material blessings

We may be tempted to think of material blessings only in terms of possessions but every breath we breath is a gift of God. Every creature which has ever lived depends upon God for its existence and substance. This is true from the archangel in heaven to the smallest insect crawling along the ground. No believer would deny this but some may object, why does God seem to give more material blessings, whether in terms of possessions or health, to some rather than others?

The answer lies in the word cup. There are big cups and small cups. There are large pint mugs for tea or coffee and there are dainty cups too. Their capacities are different and it takes more to make one overflow than the other. In terms of character and endurance, we all have different capacities. Our material needs are not all the same and are very often dictated by temperament and personality. The capacity of any cup is determined by the quantity it can contain without injury to itself by bursting its sides and without loss of its contents. This is how God deals with us. He gives us what we are capable of receiving.

The problem with most of us is that we over-estimate our capacity. We want more than would be good for us. How often have people who suddenly become very wealthy by winning a lottery prize find that they cannot cope with their new fortune. Only God knows what we are able to hold and contain without injury and loss and the secret of true contentment is to trust God to give us what is good for us. If we flatter ourselves that we can handle all that God could give then we are making the same mistake as James and John who thought they could drink the same cup Jesus was to drink. Their answer was a combination of ignorance and arrogance. They did not know what their capacity was, what they could handle and endure. Is not this the problem today with many Christians? God pours into out cup, into our experience, into what we can cope with, his richest gifts but we complain. We want more and we fail to see that our cup is already overflowing.

Spiritual wisdom teaches us to recognize our capacity and therefore to regard the smallest mercies as great. By receiving all the mercies of God in our little cup we will find that we always have reason to praise God because what we have is more than what we deserve. David knew this and he knew that God always met his needs. Sometimes he met them in simple ways and sometimes in remarkable ways but he always met them. God may not send ravens to feed us as he did Elijah but he is always our Shepherd and we shall lack nothing. If we could but see what we deserve and what we have then we would also see that our cup overflows.

Spiritual blessings

Every believer who reflects upon the value of his soul and upon the magnitude of gospel salvation will not hesitate to say that spiritually his cup is overflowing. Listen to Peter in 1 Peter 1:3-5, 'Praise be to the God and Father of our Lord Jesus Christ! In his great mercy he has given us new birth into a living hope through the resurrection of Jesus Christ from the dead, and into an inheritance that can never perish, spoil or fade—kept in heaven for you, who through faith are shielded by God's power until the coming of the salvation that is ready to be revealed in the last time.' At the beginning of his second epistle Peter has the same spiritual excitement as he contemplates the richness of the blessing of salvation, 'His divine power has given us everything we need for life and godliness through our knowledge of him who called us by his own glory and goodness. Through these he has given us his very great and precious promises, so that through them you may participate in the divine nature and escape the corruption in the world caused by evil desires' (1:3-5). Paul does exactly the same at the beginning of the Ephesian letter, 'Praise be to the God and Father of our Lord Jesus Christ, who has blessed us in the heavenly realms with every spiritual blessing in Christ' (1:3).

These men saw the greatness of their salvation and appreciated the wonder of what the Lord had done for them. Whilst other men are counting their miseries every believer should be counting his blessings. David sets us an example in Psalm 103, 'Praise the Lord, O my soul, and forget not all his benefits' (v.2). What are these benefits that God fills our cup with? The whole Psalm is taken up with them and what a list they make. He forgives me, heals me, redeems me, loves me, satisfies me. He is compassionate and gracious and does not treat me as my sin deserves. This is the lot of every saved sinner and our response to such benefits should be that of Psalm 116, 'How can I repay the Lord for all his goodness to me? I will lift up the cup of salvation and call on the name of the Lord. I will fulfil my vows to the Lord in the presence of all his people' (vv.13-14). As we drink of the cup of salvation our faith is strengthened, our love for God is increased, our hope revived, holiness and sanctification are deepened, joy begins to break forth into our worship, gratitude abounds and we will not hesitate to say that our cup is overflowing. In ourselves we are nothing and have nothing but in Christ we have a full salvation. As much grace as we need in this life and as much glory as we can enjoy in the next is all contained in the salvation we now have. It is true that we have many problems and sorrows but in the presence of grace they do not prevent our spiritual cup from overflowing. We do great injury to ourselves by failing to realize the immense benefits that came to us in salvation. It started with forgiveness of sin but did not end there. The grace that Christ brings to us is inexhaustible and immeasurable. God is our Father, Jesus is our Saviour, the Holy Spirit is our Comforter, the redeemed are our brethren and heaven is our home.

When God put the cup of salvation into our hands he did not leave it empty but filled it with all that he is. There is always a fullness to our salvation and its delights continue to amaze us as we discern more and more of the depth of God's love. Our cup is overflowing, so do not be envious of the wicked who may have more money and better health than you. To envy the wicked is to envy a man who is going to hell. If you are saved, you are the child of a King. You are complete in Christ. Take what David is saying in Psalm 23 seriously and begin to realize how blest you are. Enjoy your salvation. The table is spread, your cup is overflowing and heaven awaits you.

13
He follows me

One of the great things about being a Christian is that you can be sure of the things that matter. The world has always been a place of uncertainty. Fears and doubts plague people but with the Lord as our Shepherd we can have the confidence that David so wonderfully expresses in the last verse of the Psalm.

Surely

It is clear that David had no confidence in his own abilities. He saw himself as a sheep not a lion. But he has every confidence in his Shepherd so he says, surely—it is inevitable because of the character of the Shepherd. In the light of all that he has said in the Psalm about the Lord, it would be a great ingratitude to harbour a single doubt or suspicion as to the ability or the willingness of his God to supply all his needs up to the last moment of his existence in this world and even through death into heaven. With such a God as David had certainty could be the only reasonable attitude.

David does not say that he will never fail in his faith. Neither is he claiming that he will always be obedient to God. But he does avow a great confidence that the love and mercy of God will never leave or let him fall away entirely.

His confidence is not in himself but in his Shepherd. Biblical assurance is always based firmly upon who God is and what he has done for us. A subjective assurance that depends for its strength upon how I feel, or what I do, is always going to let us down. But an objective assurance that takes its strength from the unchanging nature and being of God is an anchor for the soul. It is powerful and immovable, firm and secure.

The gospel from beginning to end is the plan and work of God. He did not plan a jigsaw of a gospel with one essential piece missing which the sinner must supply to make it complete. It was complete when God planned it and it was complete when we came as sinners to Jesus. Our coming did not make it complete but, like all the elements of gospel truth, was also part of God's plan. It is the biblical gospel that Christ not only saves us but keeps us and will one day present us spotless before the throne of God. That is the only ground of assurance but it means that we can trust implicitly the covenant-keeping God for an unfailing supply of those spiritual and eternal blessings which are indispensable to keeping us on the way of righteousness and the path of life. So when David says, surely, it is not wishful thinking but the declaration of an inevitable fact.

Goodness and mercy

David mentions two blessings that every Christian needs, goodness and love—or goodness and mercy as the Authorized Version translates it. Goodness will supply us when we are in need and mercy will forgive us when we fall into sin. Goodness follows us to provide and mercy to pardon. Here again we see the completeness of God's salvation. Goodness with its ample gifts and ceaseless providing is not enough for an erring creature who is daily contacting sin and guilt. Mercy with its pardon multiplied and its unwavering and long-suffering love is not enough for a creature who cannot nourish and sustain itself. It is goodness and mercy working together that we need and this is what the Lord gives us. Goodness, which is the bounty and benevolence of the Lord, will follow us and supply all our needs. Mercy, which is the compassion and love of the Lord will also follow us and pardon all our sins.

David is not introducing a new thought here but merely repeating what he has already said in the Psalm. He is not afraid of repetition; how else can a sinner hope to express in words the wonder of what God has done for him? Everywhere David looked he saw the goodness and mercy of God. In Psalm 100 he declares, 'For the Lord is good, and his love (mercy) endures for ever' (v.5). In Psalm 107 he calls upon all the redeemed of the Lord to 'give thanks to the Lord, for he is good; his love endures forever' (v.1). Then in Psalm 145 he declares that future generations 'will commend your works to another; they will tell of your mighty acts . . . they will celebrate your abundant goodness' (vv.4-7). David even uses the goodness and mercy of God as an argument in prayer. 'Remember, O Lord, your great mercy and love, for they are from of old. Remember not the sins of my youth and my rebellious ways; according to your love remember me, for you are good, O Lord' (Psalm 25:6-7). So when he says that goodness and mercy will follow him all the days of his life he is not simply being poetic; rather he is delighting in one of the great truths of gospel grace.

Why are goodness and mercy so often presented to us in Scripture together? It is so that we may learn to trust God and recognize that there is a heavenly and divine element to

our lives. We are called upon to exercise discipline and effort
in our spiritual walk but there is also a tremendous input
from God. Goodness and mercy are not the result of our
efforts. They are blessings sent by God to follow us. They are
not attracted to us because of anything in us. They follow
because they are sent. Like two sheep dogs at the heels of the
flock they respond to the commands of the Shepherd to
guide and lead and provide for the sheep. They come only to
a person who has known the saving grace of the Lord Jesus.
An unsaved person knows nothing of the goodness and
mercy of God. It is impossible that any verse in the Psalm
and especially verse six can be experienced by someone who
does not know that the Good Shepherd has died to save him.
This is a blessing of redemption.

These mercies follow us, so we do not have to go looking
for them. Without them we could not exist spiritually and
prayer and assurance and trust would only be empty super-
stitions. It is these that give substance to our Christian life
and so God does not leave their functioning to the whim of
our desires. He sends them and they follow us every day of
our life.

All the days

When we became Christians Jesus did not only become our
Saviour, he also became our guarantee of a better covenant
(Hebrews 7:22). Christ as our guarantee or surety undertakes
to pay fully all our debts and fulfil every demand the law of
God requires from our sin. An example of the guarantee is
seen in Paul's words to Philemon on behalf of Onesimus, 'If
he has done you any wrong or owes you anything, charge it
to me. I, Paul, am writing this with my own hand. I will pay

it back' (vv.18-19). This guarantee exists in our good times and bad times because it does not depend upon us, but upon Christ who gives the guarantee. When we realize this it is not difficult to believe that God's goodness and mercy will follow us all the days of our life. Even when we sin they do not cease following and ministering. So don't limit this promise of God. All the days of my life simply mean every day—days when I feel the Lord to be close to me and days when I wander away from him.

The Christian is always battling in his mind with the question of merit. Most people believe in salvation by works and find the truth of salvation by grace alone to be foreign to their whole thought process. The Christian has been delivered from such thinking and rejoices in salvation by grace, but he still may have difficulties in thinking of God dealing with him only in terms of grace. Even though he knows that he is saved by grace, he may think that somehow he has to earn God's blessings and favour in his life as a Christian. Whilst the Bible rightly demands to see works as the result of faith, the Lord does not bless us not because of those works but because of his grace and love. This being the case there is no situation in which we can justly feel that God's goodness and mercy have forsaken us, because we never did deserve them. David no more deserved the blessings of God fighting Goliath than he did when he repented after sinning with Bathsheba. In fact his sin with Bathsheba would have been the end of this man unless goodness and mercy had followed him to bring him to repentance. Psalm 51 is a monument to goodness and mercy.

If the Lord is your Shepherd then you do not have to question whether or not goodness and mercy are following you—they are. They follow us in every circumstance and situation that confront us: the joys and the sorrows, the mountain top experiences and the depths of sin. They do not condone our sin. Far from it, they make us feel guilty and uncomfortable in our rebellion. They tear our conscience to shreds in order to bring us back in repentance to the Shepherd. They never stop following us if we really are God's sheep.

14
He takes me
home to heaven

Psalm 23 is pre-eminently a Psalm of privilege. It speaks throughout of what God does for his people. We noted at the beginning of this book that David is not praying in this Psalm, he is not asking God to do something for him. Rather he is rejoicing in what the Lord has done and continues to do in his life. Almost everything he mentions he has already experienced. The one exception is death but his confidence in God is so great that he has no fear of the valley of the shadow because the Lord will be there with him. Now in the last statement of the Psalm he looks beyond death to being with the Lord forever in heaven.

We have seen that everything in the Psalm flows inevitably from the first great statement that the Lord is my Shepherd. David now comes to the final inevitability. This is the glorious privilege which God confers upon all his believing people. He firstly admits them into his gracious presence in his church on earth, and eventually he will receive them into his glorious presence in the church in heaven. To dwell in a house implies having been admitted into favour and friendship with the owner. To dwell in the house of the Lord intimates that we will enjoy the blessing and honour that the Lord bestows upon his guests without interruption and without end.

The house of the Lord now

The house of the Lord is a biblical term denoting both the church militant upon earth and the church triumphant in heaven. David speaks of the former in Psalm 27:4, 'One thing I ask of the Lord, this is what I seek: that I may dwell in the house of the Lord all the days of my life.' He wants to enjoy the fellowship of God's people here and now in this life. But when Jesus in John 14:2 said 'in my Father's house are many rooms', he was speaking of heaven, not of the fabric of a building nor of a company of people living at the present time. On the other hand, when Jesus rebuked the money-changers for turning his Father's house into a den of thieves, he meant the building. It is the context which tells us each time what the phrase is referring to. To the Psalmist, and to most of the Old Testament people of God, the house of the Lord was the dwelling place of the Most High God. The cloud of his shekinah glory that hung over the tabernacle in the wilderness indicated that God was there. When Solomon built the temple the opening of this magnificent building was marked by the glory of the Lord filling it. God was there and everyone knew it. It was the divine presence that gave the building its importance: without God being there it was just a pile of stones. For Jacob the house of God was the place where he camped one night and met with God. He said, 'How awesome is this place! This is none other than the house of God; this is the gate of heaven' (Genesis 28:17).

In the New Testament it is clear that the church, not the building but the people, is called the house of God (Hebrews 3:6; 10:21; 1 Peter 2:5). Paul calls the church the household of God (Ephesians 2:19). He likens it to a structure built upon the solid foundation of the apostles and prophets, with Christ himself as the chief cornerstone. The church, says the apostle, is a holy temple and then he makes the glorious statement 'you too are being built together to become a dwelling in which God lives by his Spirit' (Ephesians 2:22). He speaks in 1 Timothy 3:15 of the church as God's household, the pillar and foundation of the truth. Clearly the New Testament has a very high regard for the church of Jesus Christ and so too should we.

When David talks of dwelling in the house of the Lord forever he was not just referring to heaven. Forever means now, at this present time as well as for all eternity. So David was glad when someone suggested to him that they go to the house of the Lord (Psalm 122:1). He saw the privilege and blessing of being there and if given the choice he would rather be a doorkeeper in the house of his God than be anywhere else (Psalm 84:10). David's attitude is one we ought to copy. It has got to be spiritually healthy for a Christian to have a high regard for the church. It may have many problems and faults but if it is God's church, if God is loved there and his truth is proclaimed there, then we ought to value it as part of God's mercy to us. When we go to church it is not to admire the architecture or to enjoy the music but to meet with God. So we prepare our hearts in private to meet with God in public. When we do so we understand the Psalmist's longing, 'My soul yearns, even faints for the courts of the Lord; my heart and flesh cry out for the living God . . . Blessed are those who dwell in your house' (vv.2,4). David had this passionate longing to be in God's house and was not disappointed when he went there, for he exclaims, 'Blessed is the man you choose and bring near to live in your courts! We are filled with the good things of your house, of your holy temple' (Psalm 65:4).

If we went to church with the same attitude what a transformation it would make to the services. Our worship would be sweeter and what we would obtain from the preaching would be more satisfying.

The house of the Lord forever

Forever does not start when you die but it does go on beyond the grave and David had his eye on greater things than are possible to experience here and now. In Paul's language, he was concerned with a house not built by hands, eternal in the heavens (2 Corinthians 5:1). When a Christian, by death, bids farewell to the house of God, his spiritual home and friends on earth, he has another home awaiting him above. There he meets again with friends and loved ones who have gone on ahead of him. He joins the company whose names are not only written in heaven but whose eternal spirits are there as well. There are very few long and detailed passages in the Bible about heaven. The reason for this is that God is not so much concerned to give us a detailed picture of heaven as to tell us how to get there. Nevertheless there are times when the Lord pulls back the curtain a little to give us a glimpse of our eternal home.

The most wonderful thing the Bible has to say about heaven is that we shall see Jesus (1 John 3:2). To the Christian, the one saved from death and hell, Jesus is everything. Peter said that to believers Jesus is 'precious' (1 Peter 2:7). But even this is an inadequate word to describe how the Christian feels about his Saviour. The hymn-writers express this feeling so well: 'How sweet the Name of Jesus sounds/In a believer's ear!' (John Newton). 'Jesus, the Name high over all' (Charles Wesley). 'Jesus, the very thought of Thee/With sweetness fills my breast' (Bernard of Clairvaux). All believers know and share these sentiments, therefore it is inevitable that to them the most wonderful thing about heaven is that they will see Jesus face to face.

Seeing Jesus inevitably promotes worship, and worship is the preoccupation of the saints in heaven. John in Revelation 5 hears the redeemed in heaven singing a new song, 'Worthy is the Lamb, who was slain, to receive power and wealth and wisdom and strength and glory and praise' (v.12).

One of the consequences of Jesus being precious to the Christian is that the believer is a person always conscious of his own sin. This is not morbid, it is the result of grace working in his life. Jesus died to deliver us from sin's bondage, yet we still sin and we know that each act of sin grieves our Saviour. So the Christian hates sin. He hates his proneness to wander from God, his sinful thoughts and spiteful actions. He longs to be free from sin and be like Jesus. That longing is finally and totally satisfied in heaven. John tells us not only that we will see Jesus but we will be like him (1 John 3:2). Now we struggle with sin and fail so often to lead a holy life. We cry with Paul, 'What a wretched man I am! Who will rescue me from this body of death?' (Romans 7:24). Such a lament is right and proper. We are to go on with the struggle but there are times when we wonder if it is all worth it. It is, because we shall see Jesus and be like him. No more sin. No more defeats by the Devil. The victory in Christ will be complete.

The absence of sin and pain and sorrow are all delights of heaven but it is what is present there more than what is absent that brings the greatest joys. One of these is the presence of complete understanding. It is only in heaven that we shall realize the massive extent and depth of the love of God.

In this world even the most blessed moments of fellowship with God are blemished by sin, but not then. The scales which mar our vision will vanish and in the words of Robert Murray M'Cheyne:

> When I see thee as thou art,
> Love thee with unsinning heart,
> Then, Lord, shall I fully know,
> Not till then, how much I owe.

Our understanding now of the perplexities of life are very confused and we are often baffled by the things which happen to us. Many circumstances come into our lives which we fight against, pray against, complain about and rebel over, but in heaven we will discover that all things have been working together for our good. These are some of the delights of the house of the Lord and they will be ours forever.

The ultimate goal

Why is the Lord our Shepherd? Why does he make us lie down in green pastures? Why does he restore our souls when we go astray? Why does he constantly seek to lead us in the path of righteousness? It is because he has an ultimate goal for us. We are saved to dwell in the house of the Lord forever.

In Psalm 23 we hear the sheep talking about the Shepherd but in John 10 we find the Good Shepherd talking about his sheep. He says, 'My sheep listen to my voice; I know them, and they follow me. I give them eternal life, and they shall never perish; no-one can snatch them out of my hand. My Father who has given them to me, is greater than all; no-one can snatch them out of my Father's hand. I and the Father are one' (vv.27-30). Our confidence in getting to heaven is not based upon arrogance or presumption but on the Shepherd's promise that he has given his sheep eternal life, and to underline that he adds the words, 'and they shall never perish'. And then to underline this truth yet again, Jesus said twice, no one can snatch them out of my or my Father's hand.

For the believer not to get to heaven and to dwell there forever, two impossible things would have to happen. First, Christ would have to fail to keep his promise and also fail to fulfil the assignment God had given him to keep eternally safe all the redeemed (John 6:37-40). Secondly, God the Father would have to fail to hold secure all those in his hand. In other words the security of the sheep depends upon the character and power of the Shepherd. The ultimate goal is set by him and guaranteed by him. For us to dwell in the house of the Lord forever is not merely a possibility, it is an inevitability. That is the strong confidence of those who with David can say, the Lord is my Shepherd.

Other books by the author
published the Evangelical Press of Wales

I Will Never Become a Christian examines the arguments and excuses of the convinced unbeliever. 'An excellent tool for evangelism'—*Covenanter Witness*.

Seeking God, written for the earnest seeker after faith. 'A welcome addition to our sparse stocks of good evangelistic material'—Robert Sheehan in *Grace* magazine.

All Things New. 28 one-page studies of 'basics of the Christian life'. 'Superb!'—*Grace* magazine.

Walk Worthy, for those who have just started on the Christian way (a sequel to *All Things New*). 'I have only words of praise for this little work. It deserves a wide circulation' Malcolm H. Watts in the *Banner of Truth* magazine.

Stand Firm, a young Christian's guide to the armour of God.

Our Present Sufferings. Biblical principles to guide us in our approach to suffering, illustrated by five testimonies from Christians who have known times of real trial and testing. 'A good booklet to place in the hands of Christians suffering from bereavement or serious chronic illness'—*Evangelicals Now*.

Firm Foundations (with Owen Milton), a two-month Bible study course introducing the new Christian to some of the great chapters of the Bible.

Christian Handbook, a straightforward guide to the Bible, church history and Christian doctrine. 'This is a book which should be widely available'—*Banner of Truth* magazine.